THE
LOST PLATES OF LAMAN

To Tiffanie —

Best Wishes —

Bob Lovett

THE
LOST PLATES OF LAMAN

AN ACCOUNT WRITTEN BY

THE HAND OF LAMAN

UPON PLATES OF TIN
MADE BY HIS OWN SELF—WITH A LITTLE
HELP FROM HIS BROTHER LEMUEL

Published by
Signature Books
Salt Lake City, Utah, U.S.A.
1997

First English edition published in 1997

© 1997 by Signature Books. All rights reserved
Signature Books is a registered trademark of Signature Books, Inc.
Printed and bound in the United States.
02   01   00   99   98   97   6   5   4   3   2   1

Library of Congress Cataloging-in-Publication Data
Lewis, Bob
The lost plates of Laman / by Bob Lewis.
p.   cm.
ISBN 1-56085-097-3 (pbk.)
1. Book of Mormon—Parodies, imitations, etc.
2. Mormons—Humor.   I. Title.
PN6231.M675L49   1997
813'.54—dc21   97-33412
                                    CIP

INTRODUCTION

Laman has always gotten bad press. True, he was a dolt. He saw angels, he heard the voice of the Lord, he witnessed miracles, and he still didn't get it! Undoubtedly you have always asked yourself, How could anybody be so dense, so indefatigably wicked?

At last, in his own words, Laman tells his side of the story. Here is the Laman you always wondered about. Here is the consummate malcontent, revealing all, holding nothing back—allowing readers a glimpse at his multi-phobic personality. Perhaps you will even sympathize with him as he describes his adolescent humiliations, the injustices he suffered at the hands of his siblings—particularly the two younger ones—and the painful neglect of a father who always favored his righteous son, Nephi, over his corrupt older brother.

Here, in vivid detail, meticulously translated from plates of tin, made by his own hands, with the help of his brother Lemuel, Laman recounts the events of his unhappy childhood, revealing the story of a sensitive boy uprooted from his home and a life of idle pleasure and forced to wander for years in the desert, eating raw meat and sleeping on the ground, coerced into sailing half way around the world on a home-made boat with only a one-way ticket, then made to live in a promised land that was totally off the grid.

Through all his sufferings and afflictions, his trials and tribulations, emerges the portrait of one who mastered the art of murmuring as few have, who left as a legacy a rich mosaic of misunderstandings, and whose hardness of heart can never be questioned.

Yes, here is the enigmatic but at last lovable Laman, the man with the unflinching and steadfast faith in the arm of flesh. —Bob Lewis, translator, October 1997

* * * * * * *

Publisher's note: The plates of Laman came into Bob's hands quite by chance as he was repairing a corrugated tin roof on a barn in Cache Valley, Utah. How the plates ended up as part of the decaying and rusted roof remains a mystery. They were not, contrary to rumors that have been circulated, purchased from Mark Hofmann, though there is considerable textual evidence that the record is not as old as it is purported to be. There has been, at the time of publication, no carbon dating of the actual tin.

THE BOOK OF LAMAN

An account of Laman and his wife Morona and his brother Lemuel and his other brothers Nephi and Sam and several relatives and even an exchange student. Father Lehi suffers from Babylonia-phobia and hauls his whole family out of Jerusalem for a long vacation near the Red Sea. Like with most vacations, Lehi forgets things. The boys go back on a wild goose chase to try to borrow some plates from their uncle Laban. Blood is not thicker than water. Laman learns about seeds, and we're not talking barley. Ishmael and a whole gaggle of daughters join the expedition. An account of their suffering and their wandering and their wading. After a lot of beach, they finally get to the surf. Nephi grows restless and goes into the boat-building business. They sail into the sunset and discover a promised land. The family splits up, and Laman reigns as king. The Lamanites and the splinter group don't get along. An account of their wars and contentions, and so forth. This is according to the account of Laman; or in other words, I, Laman, wrote this record.

CHAPTER 1

Laman fabricates his tin plates—He tells of his good life in Jerusalem and his prospects for a dandy inheritance—His father, Lehi, ruins everything by having bad dreams and then telling everybody about them.

I, LAMAN, having been born of restless parents whose motto was: a rolling stone gathers no moss; wherefore, they never really understood me, for I suffered from motion sickness as a child; therefore, they favored my younger and more righteous brother, Nephi, who liked to travel and whose account of our days he has taken upon himself to write, probably to annoy me because I was the eldest son, and partly because he knows how easily I gag at history and genealogy.

2 Now, behold, I was taught somewhat in the learning of our father, tho I never cared beans for geography and really hated inscribing; nevertheless, knowing that my younger brother was secretly scribbling away on his one-sided version of our nomadic life, therefore, I make mine own account to more or less set the record straight.

3 Yea, I write my account in ordinary language, not in the rickety and hard-to-learn language of those weird Egyptians, for I never liked the Egyptians much, and I like reformed Egyptians even less; yea, I hope to high heaven that their lingo will never become the official language.

4 And now, concerning these plates upon which my account is engraved, behold, they are made of tin, for with mine own hands did I make them, with some help from my brother Lemuel; wherefore, they are your down-to-earth practical blue-

collar plates and none of those highfalutin gold plates; yea, why waste gold as writing paper when your regular tin works fine, and then put your gold into something useful like coins or jewelry.

5 Now it came to pass that our family dwelt at Jerusalem, living in the lap of luxury, so to speak, for my father, Lehi, was a well-healed merchant and trader; wherefore, he did sock away considerable gold and silver and property; yea, but not too much, as my brother Lemuel was fond of saying, for we did enjoy living high on the hog.

6 Now as I understood it, according to our custom, a father's wealth passes to his sons after this manner: two-thirds to the eldest son, one-third to the second son, and the rest equally divided among the remaining sons. Now I, Laman, was the eldest son and lucky heir to the bulk of my father's wad, which put me on the sunny side of the tent, and I did look forward to squandering a bit of my inheritance the old fashioned way; yea, I did plan to eat, drink, and be exceedingly merry.

7 But behold, in the first year of the rain[a] of Zedekiah, king of Judah, or maybe it was in the second year, anyway a whole slew of prophets came forth prophesying; yea, Jerusalem was just oozing prophets saying unto the good people of our city that they must repent and turn from their wicked ways or their great city would be destroyed; wherefore, my brother Lemuel and I did throw rocks at the prophets, for we did not like our friends to be spoken ill of by these itinerant grouchy old men.

8 And it came to pass that my father, Lehi, did get caught up in the excitement, but instead of launching a few boulders himself and enjoying the persecution, he did take sides with the grumps; yea, he did also believe that the local wogs were wicked and that our great city was going to be wiped out; wherefore, he did tell everybody he bumped into, even our next-door neighbors and close friends, that it was time to slip on the good old sackcloth and ashes, which was not exactly in style.

9 Now when the Jews heard these things, they became angry with my father; and behold I, Laman, was a little miffed too, and my brother Lemuel also, for nobody likes a grouch, and people just naturally hate to be told that they are wicked and about to be destroyed; wherefore, we did plead with our father that he should stay at home or spend more time at the office and not annoy people by trotting out their abominations.

10 And it came to pass that I could not reason with our father, for he was as stubborn as an ox, being of the tribe of Joseph; yea, he did say unto me that he had prayed concerning these things and that a pillar of fire appeared unto him on a rock; and he did tell of many other dreams and visions.

11 And behold, Lemuel and I

---

[a]Original spelling has been retained.

did begin to worry about our father; yea, Lemuel did wonder if he might have a glandular disorder; wherefore, I did speak unto my mother, Sariah, and inquire when Lehi had his last physical; but behold, she did believe the ravings of my father, and my younger brothers and sisters also; yea, and I did begin to think that the whole family was daft; and behold, they did rebuke me, reminding me that God did appear regularly unto Moses and other prophets; wherefore, I did remind them that we were not talking about Moses but about our own flesh and blood father, Lehi, and that we were living in the rain of Zedekiah, for Pete's sake, and not way back in the dark ages, wandering in the wilderness with the thirteen tribes!

12 Now, I, Laman, do not give you the whole ball of wax, for my father said much (too much, according to my brother Lemuel); wherefore, I make a record of mine own words, plus a few clever things I wish I had thought of at the time; and behold, I give an account of how fate dealt me a flimsy hand; yea, these tin plates show that life is unfair and nasty, brutish, and short, and that man must depend upon the arm of flesh.

13 But, behold, I digress.

14 Anyway, my father, Lehi, did grow exceedingly bold and did claim to have peeked into the future; behold, he did see that Jerusalem should be destroyed and that many of its inhabitants should be carried away captive into Babylon.

15 Now behold, Lemuel and I were more than a little surprised by this prediction, for we did have a warm place in our hearts for Babylon, having been there on many shopping sprees; wherefore, we did not think twice about being carted off to Babylon.

16 And it came to pass that our father, Lehi, did become so obnoxious that people began to laugh and chuck stones at him, and I just knew that our family business would go down the toilet and that we would become despised and unpopular and never get invited to parties.

17 Wherefore, Lemuel and I did go together and purchase a copy of *How to Win Friends and Influence People*; and behold, we did present it unto our father, hoping he would stop prophesying long enough to read it.

CHAPTER 2

Laman tries to persuade his father to stop annoying the neighbors and take a vacation—Lehi decides to pack everybody off on a camping trip into the wilderness—Laman and Lemuel rescue some of the gold and silver and precious stuff.

AND it came to pass that my father, Lehi, did not hearken unto my words or unto the words of my brother Lemuel, neither to the good advice in our self-improvement book; wherefore, he did continue both day and night to preach unto the people of our city; yea, our neighbors began to avoid us and to complain about the late hours.

2 And behold, when the threatening letters began to arrive nearly every day, I did

plead with my father to cease speaking ill of everybody, or to at least find a better word than *abominations;* yea, I did remind him that most people do not like to hear that they are about to perish by the sword or to be carried away captive, even to a fun place like Babylon.

3 And it came to pass that I did pull out all the stops; yea, I did insist that he take a break from his strenuous prophesyings and enjoy himself a little and travel, even visit the Red Sea maybe.

4 Now behold, I did speedily repent of my suggestion, for it came to pass that my father did call his family together and did declare unto us that the Lord had commanded him, even in a dream, that he should pack up the whole fam and zip off into the wilderness; yea, even to the borders of the Red Sea; wherefore, Lemuel did tell me to keep my big mouth shut in the future!

5 For crying out loud, I, Laman, and also my brother Lemuel, did not wish to go hiking off into the wilderness; yea, we hated camping; wherefore, we did urge our father to pack up the others of our family, which consisted of my mother, Sariah, my younger brothers ,Nephi and Sam, our sisters, two cousins, and an unmarried aunt, and depart into the wilderness without us.

6 But behold, Lehi declared that he had been commanded to haul everybody off, including Lemuel and me, for Jerusalem was about to be destroyed; wherefore, he was throwing in the sponge; yea, he did plan to abandon his house, leave his property, even his gold and silver and precious things, and bolt, without even so much as a going away party.

7 And it came to pass that I did plead with my father to hold his horses; yea, I did reason with him, saying that it might make sense to allow me to stay behind, that I might give a detailed report concerning the destruction of our city, maybe even snap a few pictures to show some of our wickedest neighbors perishing by the sword; for behold, I could give unto him an eye-witness account of the inhabitants screaming in terror as they were carted off captive into Babylon and wishing they had heeded the handwriting on the wall, or at least the graffiti my father, Lehi, had slopped around.

8 And it came to pass that my brother Lemuel, who did claim to speak a smattering of Babylonian, did offer to remain with me, saying that together we might use our cunning craftiness to preserve our gold and silver and property from those greedy old Babylonians.

9 But behold, my father said that we were fools, for we would be killed by our own people and not by the ruddy Babylonians, and what good would our gold and silver and apartment rentals be unto us if we were dead?

10 Now behold, my father did make a good point, and after some large rocks were hurled thru our windows and my favorite araba was stripped of its wheels late one night, I did begin to believe the warnings of

my father; wherefore, we did start packing.

11 But behold, it did seem wasteful and nearsighted to leave expensive and fancy things that we could easily pack; wherefore, my brother Lemuel and I did conceal much gold and silver and other precious things among our provisions; yea, to make room we did chuck out some of the seeds and tools and supplies that our father commanded that we bring.

12 Yea, we did pull the wool over the eyes of our wasteful father and our brothers, for we did prepare for a time when we should come again unto Jerusalem, knowing that things would cool down once we got Lehi off the roof and out of town, and our sleepy neighbors were not reminded night and day about their abominations; and behold, upon our return we might once again enjoy the gold and silver and gifts from Niemann Marcus that we had so cunningly hidden away.

13 And it came to pass that we did skip out in the dead of night, and our neighbors were glad to see us go, no doubt, tho nobody came out to see us off.

14 Now behold, we did travel south toward the Red Sea, and I was sorry I had been such a klutz in geography, for I was always turned around, and my father did keep to the borders of the trade routes; wherefore, we did stay pretty much in the wilderness, which—let me tell you—was mostly sand and no picnic.

15 And I, Laman, did struggle, and my brother Lemuel also, for our camels were weighed down with about a ton of gold; wherefore, we did grumble unto our father, Lehi, for he did press forward for three days, stopping only for short rests at night, which was a lousy beginning to our vacation; yea, and Lemuel did ask again and again if we were almost there.

16 And it came to pass that we finally came to a valley by the side of a river of water, and no one had the foggiest notion where we were, tho I was sure it was no health resort, for there were no tourists there but us.

17 And my father dwelt in a tent, for once a scoutmaster, always a scoutmaster; but behold, I had left my tent in Jerusalem, having no room among my provisions; wherefore, I, Laman, and my brother Lemuel also, did sleep out in the open under the stars; yea, and I did catch a beastly cold.

18 And it came to pass that my father commanded that we should gather rocks together that he might build an altar and make an offering unto the Lord; wherefore, we did spend all day trying to find a few measly rocks, for the place was just leaking sand; yea, and I, Laman, could see no reason in it, for here we were, stuck in the middle of nowhere, and probably lost, far from our goose-down beds, sleeping on bare ground and eating take-out food?

19 Now behold, we should be thankful for that.

20 And it came to pass that in his spare time my father began to give names unto the landmarks in the wilderness, and he

LAMAN 2:21–3:2

did call the river Laman, after me, saying: Laman, be thou like unto this river, continually running, or something like that, for the words of my father did often go in one ear and out the other.

21 And behold, my father did name the valley in which we dwelt after my brother Lemuel, saying: Be like unto this valley, without moving, which I thought was perfect for Lemuel who generally sat around like a bump on a log.

22 Now behold, we did suspect that our father had been too long upon his camel, for he did command one son to be continually running, like unto a river, and the other to be immovable, like unto a valley.

23 And it came to pass that I, Laman, and also my brother Lemuel, did go again to our family on the sly; yea, we did try to convince them that Lehi was not well, and that his dreams and visions were a little too radical; wherefore, we did suggest that we might all return at once unto Jerusalem to seek professional help, and behold, Lemuel did know of a good psychiatrist with reasonable rates.

24 And it came to pass that our father got wind of our murmuring; yea, he did speak harshly unto me, and also unto my brother Lemuel; wherefore, we did suspect that our youngest brother, Nephi, was the one who had squealed on us, for at the first faint sound of a murmur he would shin off pell-mell to our father; and behold, we did decide that we would have to be more careful about where we did our murmuring.

25 Now behold, we did gripe unto our little brother about being such a tattle-tale, but he did rebuke us, saying that the trouble was with us and with the hardness of our hearts.

26 And I, Laman, did laugh at my brother, for behold, my heart is not one bit harder than my head; yea, and I am not about to believe in things I cannot see, neither in goofy dreams about events down the road, especially a dirt road.

CHAPTER 3

Laman and his brothers are sent on a wild goose chase to fetch the brass plates of Laban—They find Jerusalem still standing and nary a Babylonian in sight—Laman discovers something about genealogy and finds out that his Uncle Laban is a creep.

AND it came to pass that my father spake unto us, saying: Behold, I have dreamed a dream. And I, Laman, and my brother Lemuel did fear the worst. Why could not our father have dreams like everybody else; yea, dreams of being chased or of falling or of not being prepared for a final exam; but behold, the dreams of our father were always commands from the Lord, which always spelled trouble!

2 But lo and behold, to our surprise, this dream commanded us to return unto Jerusalem; wherefore, I, Laman, and my brother Lemuel also, did jump for joy; for behold, we were already sick of life in the wilderness, and our gold and silver and precious things we had hidden away were not worth a tinker's damn in the

valley of Lemuel beside the river of Laman; yea, we longed for the good old flesh pots of Egypt, so to speak.

3 Now behold, our joy was short and sweet, for there was more to our father's dream; yea, there always was, as Lemuel said, and the last part was always the kicker; for behold, we were commanded to go unto the house of Laban, our uncle, and to seek the genealogy of our forefathers, which was engraven upon plates of brass; yea, we were instructed to fetch those brass plates and lug them all the way back to the wretched valley of Lemuel; wherefore, my back ached and my feet hurt just thinking about it.

4 Now I, Laman, did not care scat for genealogy of any kind; wherefore, I did speak unto my father, saying that brass plates were about the last thing we needed in the wilderness, for we did not even bring our best china; yea, and if Lehi wished to study the genealogy of our forefathers, it could be done easier in the comfort of our home in Jerusalem, or better still, with our gold and silver and precious things we could hire somebody else to do our genealogy for us.

5 But behold, our father Lehi was a visionary man, and he did stick to his guns when it came to the commandments of the Lord.

6 And it came to pass that I, Laman, did murmur unto my father again, saying: I know that the Lord would give no commandment unto the children of men that was so unreasonable; yea, if the Lord was in such a rush for us to have the brass plates, could not the Lord command Laban to deliver them unto us, or have them sent express mail?

7 But behold, my father would not listen to reason; yea, he was like unto a broken record, telling us over and over again what to do until we did it; wherefore, he did insist that we should tramp clear back to Jerusalem as the Lord had commanded and fetch the heavy old brass plates and haul them all the way down here to the boondocks.

8 And it came to pass that we did set out for Jerusalem, but not before I, Laman, and also my brother Lemuel, did secretly gather together the gold and silver and valuables that we had hidden away, that we might enjoy some jolly times back in Jerusalem, for we did hope to forget the miseries of camping out; yea, as Lemuel said, the word "wilderness" did always have a rather forlorn and gloomy connotation.

9 Now, when we came again unto Jerusalem, behold, it was still standing and its people had not been shuffled away into Babylon; wherefore, I began to guffaw and to make sarcastic remarks about the foolish dreams and predictions of our father.

10 And our brother Nephi did rebuke me, for he did fully believe the words of our father that Jerusalem would yet fall and its people would yet be carried away into bondage; but behold, he could not give us a very precise date; yea, how convenient to always predict things

way off in the future, which I pointed out is the main drawback with most prophecies.

11 But behold, Sam did pipe up, saying that it is the very nature of prophecies to deal with the future, for it would be stupid to prophesy about the past. Now behold, I was much taken back by the words of Sam, for he had never spouted off before this; yea, Lemuel and I had always thought that he was more or less verbally challenged.

12 Then lo and behold, Nephi did drop another bombshell, saying that the Lord had made known the truth of these things unto him.

13 Now I, Laman, did laugh at Nephi for his foolishness, and Lemuel did nearly bust a gut; yea, I did ask Nephi why the Lord did not make these things known unto me and unto Lemuel also, or unto our old neighbors in Jerusalem who, as Lemuel did remark, might have wanted to take out a nice, fat insurance policy before the Babylonians turned up.

14 Wherefore, Nephi did remind us that the Lord had tried to make these things known unto the people of Jerusalem through his prophets, but that no one would listen; yea, and he would make the truthfulness of these things known unto me, and unto Lemuel also, if we would but ask.

15 Now behold, I spake unto Nephi, saying: Why in the world should I ask to know of something that I believe to be so goofy; yea, why would the Lord nominate a bunch of people to be his chosen folks and have them poke around all over Mt. Cyanide and then, after I don't know how long, escort them into a promised land and command them to build the great city of Jerusalem, then turn around and let a pack of heathens make mince meat out of them or truck them off into captivity?

16 Now, you tell me, does that make sense?

17 But behold, Nephi and Sam did steadfastly refuse to listen to reason; wherefore, they did insist that we perform the labor that our father had commanded, namely, to obtain the brass plates at the house of Laban; yea, I could not convince them otherwise, despite my constant murmuring, which I did gradually perfect.

18 And it came to pass that I, Laman, could see no escape from this lousy mission; wherefore, I did tell my brothers that we should cast lots to see which of us should go in unto the house of Laban; yea, and we did cast lots, and—wouldn't you know it—with my crummy luck the lot fell upon me; wherefore, I did suggest to my brothers that we should draw again, two out of three.

19 But behold, they were not in a gaming mood; wherefore, I had to go in unto the house of Laban, and behold, when I arrived, I spake unto him as he sat at meat; yea, he bade me sit far across the room from him, for he could tell that I had been some time in the wilderness and he did not wish to lose his appetite. And behold, as we spake one unto another, he did inquire of my father, which gave me the opening I wanted.

20 Now behold, I did explain that my father was traveling in the wilderness upon the advice of his physician, and that during his vacation he had become exceedingly fond of genealogy, and that now he had need of the records which were engraven upon the plates of brass, and that if Laban could spare them for a short time, we would be grateful; yea, and I myself would trot out the brass polish and shine them up before I brought them back, that they might be as good as new.

21 And it came to pass that Laban became angry, for his dinner must have gone cold, neither did he wish to part with those dusty old records. Now behold, I, Laman, was surprised to see how genealogy arouses men's passions; yea, Laban began to shout, saying that I was a thief, and he did remind me that I had once borrowed a saw which I had neglected to return.

22 Now behold, Laban became so riled that he hurled a fork at me; wherefore, I did flee out of his presence and returned unto my brothers, telling them that Laban had nearly killed me, for I did stretch the truth somewhat, saying that the fork had been a knife, and an ugly big one. Now I, Laman, began to hope in my heart that at least one inhabitant of Jerusalem would be carried away captive into Babylon, namely that scoundrel Laban.

23 And I began to be exceedingly sorrowful, for our return unto Jerusalem was not all that I had expected; yea, I did realize that you can't go home again, and I did think that we should return unto our father in the wilderness; for I, Laman, did wish to tell our father what a schmuck his cousin, Laban, was, when behold, Nephi spake unto us, saying that we should not go again into the wilderness until we had accomplished the thing which the Lord had commanded.

24 But behold, I, Laman, did remind Nephi that we were not all unanimous in our belief that this wild goose chase was cooked up by the Lord; wherefore, I did invite *him* to go in unto Laban and panhandle for the brass plates; yea, and Lemuel did urge Nephi to be firm and tell Laban to just hand over the plates and no one would get hurt.

25 But Nephi did not wish to go unto Laban, for my story must have brought him to his senses; wherefore, he did propose that we should go down unto the land of our father's inheritance, which was in the suburbs, and obtain the gold and silver and whatnot that we had left behind and lug it back here and give it unto Laban in exchange for the plates of brass.

26 Now I, Laman, began to see that truly genealogy drives people insane; wherefore, I spake sharply unto Nephi, saying that the plates were merely brass, for heaven's sake, and that we were looney to give up good gold and good silver and nice precious things for some plain old brass plates, neither did he know that a healthy portion of the family's loot was already hidden away inside our luggage.

27 But behold, Nephi did insist that it was wisdom in God that we should preserve unto our children the language of our fathers written upon these records; but behold, I, Laman, did remind Nephi that the language of our fathers was old-fashioned and fuddy-duddy, not to mention hard to understand; wherefore, it were better not to inflict this old-maidy language upon our children, and I did also remind him that, at this point, we did not have any children.

28 But behold, Nephi did argue that with these records we could also preserve the words which had been spoken by the mouth of all the holy prophets since the world began; but Lemuel did view this as a liability since all those words would certainly weigh a couple of tons, and we were already short on camels.

29 And after this manner did we contend one with another until I, Laman, and my brother Lemuel also, did throw in the towel, and we did agree to go down to the house of our father; yea, we would do whatever Nephi bade us if only he would stop preaching; wherefore, we did go, knowing deep down that we would have to cough up the gold and silver and so forth that we had so carefully squirreled away.

CHAPTER 4

The deal for the brass plates goes sour—The sons of Lehi escape by the skin of their teeth—A mysterious personage tells them to return again unto Jerusalem—Is it a trick by that rascal Laban?

AND it came to pass that we went down to the land of our inheritance, and we did gather together the gold and silver and pawnable things left behind by our father; and behold, I, Laman, and also my brother Lemuel, did slip back those things that we had taken before, so that Nephi and Sam did not know that much of the family loot had been with us all the time, and thus we did fool our younger brothers.

2 And it came to pass that after we had gathered together our gold and silver and our gewgaws, we went up again unto the house of Laban. Now I, Laman, would not go in unto Laban alone; wherefore, my brothers Lemuel and Nephi and Sam went in unto Laban with me.

3 Now behold, we were in luck, for Laban was not stuffing his face, which was a good omen, for he was a real porker and spent much of his time with his legs beneath the table, yea, and often his whole body, as Lemuel was fond of saying, referring to the drinking habits of Uncle Laban. And behold, we began to lay before him our gold and silver and a few of our most nifty precious things; yea, we laid out cash on the barrelhead, saying that we would give him everything and that we desired only the paltry old brass plates containing the dreary records of the past that had probably been cluttering up his place too long already.

4 And I, Laman, was certain that Uncle Laban would accept our offer, for he did look upon our gold and our silver and es-

"Now behold, I could not wait to tell my father what a schmuck his cousin, Laban, was, for he did snooker us out of our gold and silver and precious things."

pecially our precious things with glustig eyes. But behold, Laban was an even bigger yahoo than I thought, for he did pull the old double cross on us; yea, he did suddenly call upon his servants, who were big and strong and ugly, and they did thrust us out and did chase us with swords and sticks so that we left behind everything and barely excaped by the skin of our teeth.

5 Now I did marvel at the depravity of man, even our own flesh and blood, and Uncle Laban possessed a whole lot of flesh to be depraved; yea, I, Laman, had always believed that you can dicker and haggle and drive a sharp bargain, even stretch things a bit here and there, but that once you make a deal you stick with it, unless, as Lemuel says, you could find a sharp lawyer to help you worm out of it. But this was out and out stealing, for Uncle Laban, may he perish with indigestion, had filched all of our inheritance and what did we get—the old bum's rush!

6 And it came to pass that we did hide ourselves in a cave, that the servants of Laban who came after us in hot pursuit did not find us; and behold, I, Laman, was in an ugly mood; yea, I did not desire the pokey, old brass plates in the first place, and now to lose our gold and silver, and especially our precious things, and have nothing to show for it, made my Manasseh blood boil.

7 Now behold, as I was grousing about our loss, Nephi began to speak about the wisdom of God and the holy prophets and the commandments and other cheerful stuff; wherefore, I did pick up a small stick and smote him, and Sam also, and I did immediately begin to feel better; therefore, I did smite them again.

8 And it came to pass that there was a bright flash, like unto magic, or maybe St. Elmo's fire; and behold, there stood before us a figure, and he spake unto me, saying: Do not smite your brothers with a stick; wherefore, I did reply that it was the only thing handy. But, behold, the personage was not amused; yea, he commanded me to return again unto Jerusalem with my brothers, saying that the Lord would deliver Laban into our hands.

9 Now after the person spake thus unto me, behold, he disappeared, shazzam, like unto greased lightning; yea, and I did rub my eyes in disbelief, not knowing who in blazes he was, nor where he had come from, neither where he went; wherefore, I did tell Lemuel to look behind some rocks and search all around the cave, but he could not find him.

10 And behold, Nephi said that it was an angel of the Lord and that we should go again unto Jerusalem as we had been commanded.

11 But behold, I, Laman, did suspect that it was one of the servants of Laban who had some trick up his sleeve; wherefore, I did speak unto Nephi, saying: Not so fast! Why should the Lord deliver Laban into our hands, for we do not wish to have him but only the plates of brass, and I am not even sure

about them; yea, and have I not been twice unto the house of that hippo Laban and both times been kicked out on my ear?

12 Yea, why could not the Lord keep it simple, for if these plates are so all-fired important, why not just send this will-o'-the-wisp angel unto Laban and instruct the old goat to cough up the plates and give us back our goods for the inconvenience?

13 And I did remind Nephi that Laban was a mighty man, with plenty of goons; yea, and he could put his hands on fifty hooligans, and we were but four, which makes terrible odds.

14 But Nephi answered and said: The Lord is mightier than Laban and all of his servants, for did he not destroy the armies of Faro in the waters of the Red Sea; wherefore, let us go again unto Jerusalem that the Lord may destroy Laban, even as the Egyptians.

15 Now I, Laman, wondered how in tarnation we could entice Laban to come with us unto the Red Sea to be drowned like those unreformed Egyptians, but Lemuel said that Nephi was speaking metaphorically; nevertheless, my heart was full of doubts as we slouched again toward Jerusalem.

CHAPTER 5

Nephi goes to the house of Laban in Jerusalem—Laman and Lemuel slip into the city for some merry making—Nephi returns wearing the armor of Laban and scares his brothers half to death—They learn that Laban has lost his head, and not metaphorically—Zoram joins the party, so Laman makes him carry the brass plates.

AND it came to pass that we did return again unto Jerusalem, and I, Laman, would not go in unto the house of Laban, for I thought I was coming down with the flu; wherefore, Nephi bade us remain without the walls of the city that we might hide ourselves.

2 And Nephi crept into Jerusalem alone, for he was a foolhardy and impetuous kid who was determined to get himself killed, and perhaps his brothers also.

3 Now behold, I, Laman, began to feel a bit better, tho I did grow weary of waiting, and my brother Lemuel also; wherefore, we did agree to sneak into the city for a little diversion; but behold, Sam, who was not exactly the life of the party, would not go with us, saying that he would wait for Nephi to return.

4 And it came to pass that as we crept into the city, behold, we stumbled upon a small inn, and within there was much laughter and merry making; wherefore, I, Laman, and also my brother Lemuel, did join the revelers and did help paint the town red, for we had enjoyed ourselves very little in the wilderness, and even less hiding in that miserable cave.

5 And as we drank and caroused and had a randy old time, spending what little gold and silver and heirlooms Laban had not stolen from us, behold, one of the elders recognized us and said that our Uncle Laban

LAMAN 5:6-16

had just departed, for he had also been out whooping it up for much of the night, thanks, no doubt, to the gold and silver and trinkets he had pinched from us.

6 Now, fearing that some of the servants of Laban might recognize us also, we did depart in haste, but not before buying everybody a drink and putting the entire bill upon the tab of Laban, curse his hide.

7 And when we returned without the walls of the city, behold, Sam was waiting for us alone, for Nephi had not yet come back; yea, I did suspect that he might never come back, for if that cranky Laban was stormy when he was sober, he was positively typhoonish when he was in his cups.

8 And it came to pass that as we told Sam of our narrow escape, for Lemuel did throw in a few colorful embellishments, behold, we beheld Laban his own self approaching us with his armor gird about his loins, and he was also bearing his sword; wherefore, we were in trouble, for we didn't even have a lousy flipper; yea, and one of Laban's servants was limping along after him.

9 Now we did suppose that Laban had slain Nephi and did seek to throttle us as well; wherefore, we did take to our heels.

10 But behold, a voice did call unto us, and it was the voice of Nephi; wherefore, we did cease to flee. Now I, Laman, did smell a trap; therefore, as a precaution, I did send Sam and also Lemuel to speak unto Laban or Nephi or whoever it was with the armor gird about his loins.

11 But now the servant of Laban began to turn tail and run, for behold, it was Nephi, our brother, in disguise, with the armor of Laban gird about his loins but looking a little baggy; wherefore, Nephi did seize the servant by the scruff of the neck and did hold him, that he should not flee.

12 And I, Laman, did rejoice that Nephi had somehow gotten hold of the armor and the sword of Laban, for I did immediately notice that the armor was of exceedingly fine workmanship, and the hilt of the sword was of pure gold; yea, it was a good beginning to replace at least some of the precious stuff swiped from us by that blimp Laban.

13 And I, Laman, and my brother Lemuel also, did inquire of Nephi, asking if he had salvaged any of our gold and silver or precious do-dads from that sleaze-bag Laban.

14 And it came to pass that Nephi did relate unto us the events of the night within the city; wherefore, he did explain that as he crept forth unto the house of Uncle Laban, behold, he found a man who was as drunk as a fiddler, and behold, as luck would have it, there lay dear old Laban.

15 Now Nephi did believe that the Lord had delivered our uncle into his hands; wherefore, he did cut off the head of Laban with his own sword; yea, and Lemuel did make a sick joke about us not being the only ones who did paint the town red.

16 And I, Laman, did thank the Lord that he did answer my

curses; wherefore, I did marvel at the wisdom of the Lord, for it did seem much cleaner and more efficient to slay that lout Laban right here in his backyard rather than to haul him all the way down to the Red Sea and drown him like unto the armies of old King Faro.

17 Now behold, after Nephi had cut off the head of Laban, he took off his armor and his garments and put them upon his own body and went forth into the house of Laban.

18 And it came to pass that as he entered the house, he went forth towards the treasury; and behold, he saw one of the servants dangling a mess of keys; wherefore, Nephi spake in the voice of Laban and did snooker the servant into opening the treasury, saying that he had need of the plates of brass, for his brethren were without the walls of the city and could not wait until morning to work on their genealogy.

19 Now behold, this servant, whose name was Zoram, was somewhat thick between the ears; yea, he did think that Nephi was his master, even though the armor was very saggy and the impression Nephi gave of Laban would not have fooled a half-witted sheep; wherefore, Zoram did go with Nephi and did open the treasury, for he did suppose that the brethren who wanted the brass plates were those that his master had been out with, but even a nitwit would have known that these brethren, after a night on the town, were in no condition to work on their genealogy or anything else.

20 And behold, Nephi went straight for the plates of brass, neither did he snitch any of our gold and silver and durable goods as I would have done, but he did snatch the plates and did make a bee-line for the front door and scudded off for the gates of the city, rattling along in the armor that was about two sizes too big, with Zoram shuffling along behind him.

21 Now behold, when Nephi came near unto where we were hiding and did call unto us as we fled before him, behold, Zoram began to tremble in fear, for it did finally dawn on him that this was not his master, for Nephi was a tenor; yea, and Zoram knew also that we were not the brethren waiting without the walls of the city to do our genealogy work, unless it were a little late-night work for the dead.

22 And it came to pass that Nephi spake unto him, even with an oath, saying that his life would be spared and we would let him off the hook if he would go down into the wilderness with us, and behold, Zoram did not think long about it, for he had been planning to take a little vacation time; wherefore, he did also make an oath, saying that he would go with us; yea, the oaths were just flying; wherefore, I did remove my foot from his neck, that he did stand again upon his feet.

23 Now I, Laman, spake unto my brothers, saying that we were sitting in the catbird seat, for we did have the keys to the treasury of the late Laban; wherefore, we should slip back and fetch the things that had

LAMAN 5:24-6:4

been nicked from us by the dearly departed; yea, and we should perhaps remove a few other items, like maybe a bunch of gold swords, as interest.

24 And Lemuel also did agree, saying that surely kind old Uncle Laban would want us to help ourselves to his worldly wealth since he had little need for it, having been so recently dispatched by Nephi to that great treasury in the sky; yea, why not reduce the inheritance taxes?

25 But Nephi did fear that the body of Laban would be found, and that his servants would be searching for us; yea, and if they found us, they would kill us; wherefore, he was desirous that we should high-tail it unto the tent of our father.

26 Now behold, I did wonder why in tarnation Nephi did not properly dispose of the remains, for I did hate to leave all that loot behind, especially since most of it had been mooched from us, but I did also remember clearly those surly thugs of Laban, and I did not wish to get chased again at the point of so many swords; wherefore, we did beat a hasty retreat into the wilderness, but I did insist that Zoram carry the brass plates.

CHAPTER 6

Laman and his brothers return unto the tent of Lehi in the wilderness—There is much rejoicing and thanksgiving—The contents of the brass plates are a big disappointment.

NOW, I, Laman, could see that we were in a clove hitch; for behold, we had left Jerusalem with a big, ugly cloud over us, and I do mean that hot-air balloon Laban, for his abrupt passing might be traced to us, and here we were with no gold or silver or baksheesh wherewith to bribe the judges or pay high-priced lawyers; wherefore, we were doomed to wander in the wilderness as nomads, living in tents and eating junk food and pretending to be happy because we had the plates of brass with the genealogies of our fathers; yea, it was our only reading material, and I did not even know if it had a good plot.

2 Now when we did return unto the tent of my father, behold, my father and mother did rejoice; yea, and I did rejoice also, for I had dreamed a dream that when we had returned unto the valley of Lemuel by the river Laman, lo and behold, we had found only a "For Rent" sign and our father had disappeared into the wilderness with no forwarding address.

3 And behold, my mother did suppose that we had perished in the wilderness, for she did believe that we would simply sashay up to Jerusalem, fetch the plates of brass and come galumphing back in next to no time and not stay away so long, for the days in the wilderness did drag along like a lame camel.

4 Wherefore, my mother had complained against my father, calling him a visionary man, which did show that she, at least, was coming to her senses; and behold, she did murmur that her sons had been killed, which was almost true, and she

did fear that she would also perish in the wilderness; yea, she did make it mighty uncomfortable in the tent of my father; wherefore, his joy was especially full now because of the silence of my mother.

5 Now behold, my father, Lehi, did take the records which were engraven upon the plates of brass, and he did search them from the beginning; yea, he did study them over day and night, which did waste many of our candles and a lot of his time.

6 And behold, the only things written upon the plates of brass were the books of Moses and the story of Adam and Eve and a whole slew of other ancient records, plus some genealogy; wherefore I could not see why our father had made such a fuss about them, especially since what we really needed was a good map.

7 But when my father saw all these things written upon the plates, behold, he was filled with the spirit, for it did not take much to set him off; yea, and he began to prophesy concerning his seed; and behold, I feared that he would discover that I had not packed all of the seeds he had commanded me to bring, but Nephi told me he was speaking about his children and his descendants; wherefore, I began to breathe easier; yea, I did let my mind wander to the prospects of trading the sword of Laban for some good-looking Bedouin wife.

CHAPTER 7

Laman explains the brass plates and what a nuisance they have become—He describes the purpose of his own record.

AND now I, Laman, would say somewhat concerning the brass plates of Laban, for they were a pain in the you-know-what unto us; yea, and as it turned out, an even greater headache unto Laban.

2 Now behold, the dream of my father had been exceedingly short on details, which is why we nearly lost our skins in obtaining the plates.

3 And I, Laman, believe that it was by shear luck that we were able to snake them away from the treasury of Laban, for behold, we had twice gone in unto that bloated bulk with a kosher offer, that we might obtain the plates from him in a nice, friendly manner, and twice he did bamboozle us.

4 Yea, he even sicked his servants upon us; wherefore, we were forced to hide ourselves in that smelly and cramped cave; but behold, as Lemuel did say, the third time was a charm; yea, it was only by chance that Nephi stumbled upon Laban as drunk as a skunk.

5 Now behold, we had shagged the plates, but we had also lost our gold and silver and all of our whatchamacallits, with only one crummy gold sword and some baggy armor to show for it.

6 But my father, Lehi, was as happy as a clam; yea, he declared unto us that these plates of brass should go forth unto all nations, kindreds, and the tongues of people.

7 And I, Laman, did tremble to think that we must forever carry them, like unto an alba-

tross around our necks; yea, and I did have nightmares about hauling them about the desert unto diverse and unsuspecting nomads; wherefore, I did imagine how thrilled they would be to see our book of genealogy; yea, it would be like showing pictures of the grandchildren unto total strangers.

8 And I spake unto my brother, Lemuel, asking him what our father meant, that the plates of brass should go forth unto the tongues of people, and he did explain that with some people genealogy must be shoved down their throats.

9 Now I, Laman could believe that; wherefore, I say no more about the plates of brass, for I am sick of them, neither do I include the genealogy of my fathers in mine own record, for if ever I have any children, which I doubt, I will spare them this irksome misery; yea, I do earnestly hope that they will grow up at a time when genealogy is kaput, or at least when it is more user-friendly, like family history.

10 Now behold, I do fill my record with our constant troubles and our endless sorrows and our knee-deep afflictions; in short, the things which are pleasing unto the world, for there is nothing more satisfying unto man than to hear of the misfortunes of somebody else; wherefore, the things that I write are bound to give exceeding great joy and comfort unto the children of men.

11 But behold, my inner-most thoughts and ruminations I do keep for my secret diary, which I have recorded upon other plates; yea, it did seem that everyone did get into the plate-making line, but then there isn't a whole lot to do in the wilderness, and, of course, everybody considers himself an author; wherefore, if you wish to know about our type of government, our monetary system, our foreign policy, and such deep matters, I hope you can pick up a second-hand copy of the *Medium-sized Plates of Laman.*

CHAPTER 8

Would you believe it? The sons of Lehi are sent back unto Jerusalem again—They retrieve Ishmael and his family—Laman and Lemuel schmooze the daughters of Ishmael, and they agree to journey into the wilderness to hunt for shells at the Red Sea—Bad weather brings on a whole bunch of murmuring—Nephi reviles his brothers once too often, so they tie him up—Their dilemma: should they leave him to starve or feed him to wild beasts?

AND it came to pass, but I know you will not believe it, that my father, Lehi, had another dream; yea, I did begin to wonder if he slept all the time; wherefore, he spake unto us, saying that the Lord had spoken unto him yet again, and that he was commanded that he should not take his family into the wilderness alone.

2 Now behold, I, Laman, do not mind telling you that I did begin to murmur big time, saying unto Lemuel that the Lord should jolly well make up his mind; yea, from the beginning I did think it was a crummy idea

having to go off into the wilderness alone, neither did I need anybody to tell me.

3 But behold, there was more, for my father did now reveal unto us that we should take daughters to wife, that we might raise up seed in a land of promises; and behold, as Nephi had told me before, my father was not speaking of barley!

4 Now Lemuel did interject a very good question, asking if we were commanded to take just any old daughters to wife that might be handy, or if we could, maybe, pick out the daughters ourselves, especially since our sojourn in the wilderness was likely to be pretty long and the quarters uncommonly small; wherefore, it would be easier raising seed, so to speak, if we had some say about who would do the farming with us.

5 But wouldn't you know it, this time the dream of our father was very specific; yea, the Lord had commanded us to return again unto the land of Jerusalem and to lure away the family of Ishmael, which had a whole flock of daughters, that they might enjoy this wilderness adventure with us.

6 Now behold, I did raise a question or two about this wacky idea, saying unto my father that Ishmael and his family were not entirely looney; yea, why would they just drop everything and pull up stakes and scurry off into the wilderness for a nightmare jamboree in the valley of Lemuel; yea, we did not even have any gold or silver or precious do-dads to entice them.

7 But behold, my father did not bat an eye, for when the Lord gave him a commandment, behold, he did stick to it, especially when fifty percent of his sons were born travellers; wherefore, he did boot us out of the tent and told us to hit the road for the house of Ishmael.

8 And it came to pass that this time, behold, I, Laman, did no more need a map, for I could now make the trip blindfolded; yea, I might have made good money as a trail guide if we could have found anyone nutty enuf to go into the wilderness; and behold, Lemuel did suggest we might start up a little business taking juvenile delinquents on survival courses; wherefore, Nephi did suggest that we had better just look after ourselves.

9 Now behold, Ishmael and his family were known unto my father; yea, I, Laman, and also my brother Lemuel, were quite familiar with two of the daughters of Ishmael, for we had stolen out on more than one night to meet them at a lively kabera.

10 Now the family of Ishmael consisted of five daughters and two sons and an exchange student; and behold, the sons were already married and did each have three seeds, as my father, Lehi, would have said.

11 And it came to pass that as we journeyed up unto the house of Ishmael, behold I, Laman, did worry about what we should say unto them, for I did not think that our nomadic life would go over big with the daughters of Ishmael, they being city girls: neither did I believe that old Ishmael would be exactly chomping at the bit to

LAMAN 8:12-19

light out with us for Timbuctoo.

12 But behold, Nephi spake unto us, saying that we should speak the words of the Lord unto Ishmael, and that the Lord would soften his heart; wherefore, Lemuel did mutter under his breath that it might be even better if the Lord would just weaken the old bird's head.

13 And it came to pass that we did arrive at the house; and behold, Ishmael did gather his family together to hear us, for it was as plain as the nose on your face that we had not dropped by to do home teaching; yea, we did look a little wild and wooly and smelt something fierce; wherefore, they did expect a pretty juicy story, for I did wonder if they had already heard the sad news about our dear old Uncle Laban.

14 And Nephi did relate unto them all of the events from the beginning, from the time that we first left Jerusalem; and behold I, Laman, did improve upon some of the more colorful parts; yea, and Lemuel also did embellish our story, stretching things a bit too far, in my opinion, for nobody did believe the part about how he held the cave against forty or fifty angry servants waving swords and knives.

15 And after we had told our story unto Ishmael and his family, behold, I, Laman, and my brother Lemuel, did secretly meet with the daughters of Ishmael, for I could see that they were not thrilled with the prospects of leaving home; wherefore, we did tell them how much fun the wilderness was, and that I even had a river named after me, and Lemuel did show them some pretty shells that he said came from the Red Sea, though I think he won them off some Galilean in a card game; yea, and we did convince them that we would probably come back in a few weeks anyhow, after my father, Lehi, got tired of genealogy.

16 And lo and behold, to my great surprise, Ishmael, and also his household, even their exchange student, did agree to go off with us into the wilderness; yea, after several days of packing we did shove off with the whole shebang.

17 Now behold, for two days we did meander along with much laughter and singing, for the daughters of Ishmael did look upon our journey as a chance to kick up their heels; wherefore, I, Laman, began to think that the wilderness was not as miserable as I had remembered; yea, Lemuel and I did begin to think of ourselves as tour guides.

18 But it came to pass upon the third day that there arose a nasty storm, and the sand blew into our clothing and into our eyes and into our mouths, which pretty much put a stop to the singing; wherefore, we were forced to take refuge at a tiny oasis.

19 And Ishmael did pitch his tent, and Nephi also, and all of the children of Ishmael, and took shelter from the wind and sand; but behold, I, Laman, and also my brother Lemuel, were caught short again, for we did like to travel light; wherefore, we did huddle beside some rocks to shield ourselves from

the wind and sand for what seemed a month until the storm ceased.

20 And after the storm, two of the daughters of Ishmael did come unto me, and unto my brother Lemuel, saying that they had already grown weary of life in the wilderness; yea, they did say that the wilderness stunk; and behold, they were the daughters known unto us from before; yea, and one of them did have a bad rash; wherefore, Lemuel did think we should return in haste unto Jerusalem.

21 And it came to pass that we did conspire with the two daughters of Ishmael, that we might twist the arm of their father to return again unto Jerusalem, unto the land of his inheritance, for we did secretly hope that it might also now be our inheritance since we had lost all of our own pile to that rat-fink Laban.

22 And the daughters of Ishmael did lay it on thick with their father, saying that they enjoyed the beach, but that a little water would be nice; yea, and that the sun and wind were harmful to their nice complexions, and that riding so long upon a camel would do harm unto Ishmael's kidneys; wherefore, they did butter him up, using the cunning words that Lemuel and I had hatched up together.

23 Now the sons of Ishmael did also murmur against their father and against our brother, Nephi, for they began to see that life in the wilderness was no bed of roses; yea, it was lousy soil to raise their seeds, neither did their wives and children like so much sand with so little pleasure and such small helpings of cold food from a very limited menu.

24 Now behold, I, Laman, did see that there were more who wanted to return unto Jerusalem than those who wished to continue trudging in the wilderness, that is if we counted the children and did not give a vote unto the exchange student; wherefore, I did propose that the caravan become a democracy, saying that we should abide by the decision of the majority whether we returned unto Jerusalem or kept making footprints in the sand.

25 But behold, Nephi did stand forth, and he did have that look of grief upon his countenance that came about every other day; yea, and he did revile us again for the hardness of our hearts, saying unto me, and unto Lemuel also: Behold, why must I, your younger brother, set an example unto you, and why is it ye are so hard in your hearts?

26 Now I, Laman, did not wish to look bad in front of the daughters of Ishmael; wherefore, I did stand up to my younger brother, Nephi, saying that we were sick and tired of his good example, and Lemuel did remind him that as for our hard hearts, behold, it was better than having no heart at all; yea, it was heartless to make these fair and lovely young girls wander in this sun-baked waterless wasteland.

27 And I spake forcefully unto Nephi, saying that I did not believe in the foolish imaginings of

an old man, or of a young man either, for that matter; yea, had we not returned unto Jerusalem many times (too many times, Lemuel chimed in) and found the old place safe and sound, neither were its inhabitants slain or whisked away into captivity, tho one of its elders had lost his head, thanks to Nephi and the curse upon the brass plates.

28 But Nephi stood his ground, for he was a chip off the old block, and he did insist that Jerusalem would end up beans on toast, just as the Lord had said, and that we would be the first to know about it, except for the poor Jerusalites themselves; yea, and he did chide us, saying: Did you not see an angel? Yea, and did not the Lord deliver us out of the hands of Laban, that we did obtain the record of our fathers?

29 Now behold, nobody likes to get cornered; therefore, I grew angry at my brother, saying: Do not hearken me, for if the Lord did deliver us out of the hands of Laban, who shoved us into the hands of Laban in the first place? And behold, as for this so-called angel that did scare us half to death, did he not look strangely like unto a man, and where were his wings?

30 Then Nephi spake unto us again, saying: If you are determined to return unto Jerusalem, go, and ye shall perish also; but behold, remember the words which I speak unto you by the Spirit of the Lord!

31 Now behold, this was the last straw; yea, how could Nephi think that we would be taken in by this reverse psychology, for we did now see that he had been leading us on, feeding our hatred of the wilderness so that we would wish to return unto Jerusalem to perish with its inhabitants; wherefore, we did lay our hands upon Nephi, and none too gently, I can tell you, and we did bind him with cords that Lemuel had filched from one of the sheds of Ishmael.

32 And it came to pass that Lemuel did remind me of the story of Isaac, whose brothers sold him into Egypt because he was so annoying; but behold, there was no band of hairy Midianites handy to buy Nephi; yea, and we could have used a little extra cash; wherefore, we did keep Nephi bound while we considered whether to let him slowly starve to death or leave him to be devoured by wild beasts, or possibly a nice combination of the two.

33 And it came to pass that as we labored in thought, behold, somehow Nephi got free from his bands and stood again before us; wherefore, I did smack Lemuel a good one for tying Nephi up with a granny knot.

34 Then, behold, Nephi did again speak unto us of the hardness of our hearts and did insist that it was indeed the Lord who had commanded us to do all these things; wherefore, Lemuel did give him high praise for persistency, but did mark him way down for being redundant again and again.

35 And it came to pass that we were about to pounce upon Nephi once more, but behold, one of the daughters of Ishmael

and one of the sons of Ishmael, yea, and even the wife of Ishmael did plead with us that we should not harm him, and I did half expect old Ishmael himself to say something, but he was probably off dozing in his tent.

36 And it came to pass that my majority was slipping, therefore I did listen to the pleading of our party and did promise not to leave our brother to starve in the wilderness, neither would I let him become a meal for wild beasts; and behold, to show my kinder, gentler side before everybody, I did bow down unto Nephi, and I did ask him to forgive us—especially Lemuel, who thought up the whole thing—for we did not really mean to harm him; yea, it was all done in fun, that we might break the monotony of gadding about in this boring wilderness.

37 And lo and behold, the weather did clear and the wind stopped and all our company grew happy again; wherefore, we did prepare to light out once more for the tent of my father.

38 And I, Laman, spake unto the disgruntled daughters of Ishmael, saying that roaming a few more days would do little harm and would make Nephi happy; yea, I did promise to take them fishing on the river Laman and even show them the Red Sea, if we could find it; and I did tell them that my father, Lehi, would soon have another dream, and we would be commanded to return unto Jerusalem anyway.

39 Wherefore, we did hit the road again until we did arrive at the tent of my father, and he did again give thanks unto the Lord for our return and for all of the house of Ishmael who had joined us; and behold, he did offer sacrifices and burnt offerings unto the Lord, but I, Laman, did believe he should requisition a bigger tent.

CHAPTER 9

Lehi has a nightmare: mists of darkness, an unknown river, suspicious fruit, obnoxious people, and what looks like the World Trade Center—Laman interprets the dream and sees the deep-seated anxieties and guilt pangs of his father—Never trust voices that tell you to get out of town.

AND it came to pass that we had not been many days in the valley of Lemuel beside the river Laman when my father spake unto us again, saying: Behold, I have dreamed a dream, or in other words, I have seen a vision.

2 Now behold, I, Laman, did wink unto the daughters of Ishmael, and in my best stage whisper did say: What did I tell you! Pack your bags!

3 But lo and behold, the latest dream of my father was a complete surprise, for this time we were not commanded to return unto Jerusalem; yea, this dream, or whatever, was a real humdinger.

4 Now I, Laman, do not give a full account of the dream of my father, for I cannot even remember my own dreams, except the one I have had twice concerning one of the daughters of Ishmael, neither can I recall half the things in the dream of my father, which was very

LAMAN 9:5-14

confusing, for it was filled with mists of darkness and rivers of waters and throngs of people and spacious fields and amber waves of grain, with purple mountains above fruited plains.

5 But behold, I will give you the highlights of the dream, as nearly as I recall. My father, as his dream opened, was lost in a dark and dreary wilderness for the space of many hours; yea, and Lemuel did say that he had recently dreamed this part of the dream himself, except that he had not been asleep.

6 And it came to pass that my father beheld a large field and a tree laden with some sort of white fruit, which he ate without even washing, neither did he know what variety it was; nevertheless, he did call unto my mother and my brothers, Nephi and Sam, that they might eat also; and behold, they did come unto him and did eat.

7 And it came to pass that my father yelled at me, and at Lemuel also, as he frequently did; but behold, we would not come, for there was a river of water between us and we could not swim.

8 Then my father beheld a metal rod, of brass I think, running along the path leading to the tree, and bunches of people were pressing forward, shoving and pushing; yea, even tho there was only one tree, nobody thought to queue up; but behold, a cloud of smog suddenly rolled in; yea, it was a real pea souper which thinned out the crowd considerable, for a whole mess of them let go of the rod of brass and lost their chance for a taste of the unknown fruit.

9 And it came to pass that my father spied a humongous building beyond the river, which was probably the source of the smog, and it was jammed full of people who were pointing their fingers and making other obscene gestures and laughing at those who were eating the suspicious fruit.

10 And Lehi beheld many other things which I have forgotten and cannot remember, for he must have been dreaming most of the night.

11 Now behold, after telling everybody about his dream, my father did speak somewhat harshly unto me, and unto Lemuel also, for he feared that we should be cast off from the presence of the Lord just because we would not partake of the fruit in his dream.

12 Now I, Laman, was annoyed by this, and I did complain unto my father, saying that it was his dream and not mine, for heaven's sake; yea, if I were to dream that Lemuel stole one of my camels, I would not go to him to gripe about what he did in my dream, although now that I think about it, Lemuel was probably the one who did nick one of my camels that turned up missing last spring.

13 And behold, I did begin to see that my brother Nephi, and also Sam, did think that they were better than me, and Lemuel also, just because they did scarf down the white figs, or whatever, and we did not.

14 Now behold, I, Laman, will give you my own interpretation of the dream of my father, for dreams are easy to understand if you read between the lines;

yea, as Lemuel did say, and it was just beautiful the way he did put it: Our deepest worries and anxieties and hangups are revealed through metaphors of the unconscious mind.

15 Wherefore, the dark and dreary wilderness is as plain as the nose on your face, for it is the miserable terrain we had been slogging thru for many days; yea, it was not always dark, but it was nearly always dreary.

16 Now the tree laden with fruit is as simple as pie, for it is your basic wish fulfillment; for behold, my father had been without fruit for months; yea, and he did often chide me, and my brother Lemuel also, because of our fruitless efforts; wherefore, fruit was uppermost in his mind; yea, and as Lemuel did remind me, from the time we were little our father did always force us to eat weird, high-fiber fruits and vegetables, so even in his dreams he was concerned about our intake of ruffage.

17 Yea, my father knew well that I, and Lemuel also, did swim like unto a rock, and still he did bid us come unto the tree, tho we stood across the river of waters; and behold, Nephi and Sam did not have to paddle for it, which shows that my father did always favor Nephi, and also Sam.

18 Now behold, I did see an even darker side to this dream; yea, could not the river of waters represent the river Laman, named after me; wherefore, did not Lehi subconsciously hope to see us both drown because we did not believe in his many dreams?

19 And I did confide unto Lemuel that Nephi did also wish to drown us, for he had often spoken about how Moses drowned the armies of Faro in the Red Sea, and I did see that Nephi was using transference; and behold, he was also hoping that his older brothers would drown and leave him to be the uncontested head camel.

20 But behold, Lemuel did say that I was becoming paranoid.

21 Now the rod of brass was a piece of cake, for it did clearly symbolize the obsession of Lehi with the plates of brass; wherefore, he did believe that everyone desired to cling to them; yea, those who did wander off and were lost in the midst of darkness and did not hold fast to the rod represent people who refuse to turn in their four-generation group sheets.

22 And behold, the great and spacious building is clearly downtown Jerusalem, for city people will always laugh at rubes who think they can sashay off into the wilderness without even a map or at bumpkins who can't even remember to take along their gold and silver and precious things like credit cards; wherefore, my father did hide his guilt and embarrassment about leaving his comfortable home and nice neighborhood and subjecting his family to life on the road; yea, it was classic denial.

23 Now I, Laman, have written a more or less complete interpretation of the dream in my secret diary; but behold, my brother Lemuel did say that all this inscribing was just a waste

of time anyway, for nobody would give a hoot about any of our dreams or about our gallivanting in the wilderness, neither did he like to be reminded of all our troubles, and especially the odious trip in Nephi's boat.

24 But behold, I get ahead of my story.

CHAPTER 10

Laman and Lemuel worry about their father's discourse on horticulture—Laman ponders the meaning of time.

AND it came to pass that after my father had wrapped up his stream-of-consciousness dream-scape, behold, he did launch forth again concerning the naughty Jews and poor old Jerusalem and the bloodthirsty Babylonians, et cetera, which was getting to be old hat.

2 But behold, my father did now add a new twist to the story; yea, he did explain that sometime after the great destruction of Jerusalem, behold, the inhabitants should be brought back out of captivity; wherefore, I did see that we were not the only ones whose crummy luck it was to keep on shuffling back and forth unto Jerusalem; yea, Lemuel did think the chosen people were a lot like poor old Sisyphus, whoever he was.

3 And I, Laman, did gripe about this, saying that the Lord should make up his mind; yea, it were better not to be a chosen people if the Lord keeps sending you packing all over the planet, and never first-class.

4 And it came to pass that my father did scrape together a few more prophecies; yea, he did compare the House of Israel unto an olive tree, whose branches should be broken off and scattered upon all the face of the earth; and behold, after all of this scattering, there should be a whole bunch of gathering.

5 Now I, Laman, did worry that my father had been too long inside his tent; yea, what did he, a businessman, know about farming and olive trees? And behold, if anyone was broken off and scattered abroad, it was my father and his family; yea, we had been peeled away from Jerusalem, pruned of our gold and silver and precious stuff by that sharecropper Laban, cut off from our home, with our inheritance nipped in the bud; wherefore, we had ended up being transplanted into a wilderness of sand that won't grow squat!

6 But behold, I hyperventilate.

7 And it came to pass that my father did continue to speak and to prophesy of what would come to pass; yea, he did love to rattle on about the future and the mysteries of God; but behold, nobody can understand the mysteries of God, for what's the good of having a mystery if somebody figures it out? Yea, I, Laman, do not believe we can know the future; but behold, I do wish we could, for it would be a big help unto me in my wagers with Lemuel, for either he cheats or is uncommonly lucky.

8 Now behold, I write somewhat concerning the past and the present and the future; yea, I share my wisdom with all

those who have the misfortune to read my account preserved upon these plates of tin, made by my own hands, with the help of you know who. Now I, Laman, do declare that the past is past and the future never comes; wherefore, live in the present; yea, look upon each new day as the last day of the rest of your life; for behold, if the Lord sends you wandering off into the wilderness, there is a good chance that it *will* be.

9 And it came to pass that my father did speak many more things that were hard to understand, especially since we dwelt in the valley of Lemuel, far from any library; wherefore, I, Laman, did not think they should be added unto these plates of tin to cause frustration and irritation unto our seed.

10 Now behold, the words of my father did push Lemuel to his wit's end, which wasn't very far; yea, he did come unto me for comfort, saying: What does our father mean? for first he spake unto us of fruit trees that we could not classify and rivers of polluted water, and now he speaks of olive trees and branches and grafting; yea, he did use many images from horticulture, which thing is a mystery unto me; and he did also refer again and again unto the gentiles; and behold, he knoweth that we have not learned anatomy.

11 But behold, I did console Lemuel, saying that I was also in the dark, for most of what our father said was Greek to me; wherefore, we did dispute one with another about the hard words of our father; yea, and I did explain my Freudian interpretation of the white-fruit dream unto Lemuel, but he could hardly keep from laughing, tho he could not come up with anything better.

12 And it came to pass that Nephi did come unto us with his standard look of grief upon his countenance, and he did inquire concerning the cause of our wrangling.

13 Wherefore Lemuel did speak unto him saying: We do not understand the words of our father, neither do we think his dreams of fruit and olive trees and scattered gentiles have anything to do with the price of wheat in China.

14 And behold, without asking my permission, Lemuel did tell Nephi of my nifty interpretation of the fruit dream; and behold, the look of grief upon Nephi's face did turn to pain, and he spake unto us, saying: Have ye inquired of the Lord?

15 And I, Laman, answered saying: No, we have not, for the Lord makes no such thing known unto us, neither does he make such things known unto any man, nor woman either; yea, why would the Lord bother to make rhyme or reason out of dreams which but reflect the daily events of life assembled at random in our minds during sleep?

16 And it came to pass that Nephi did chide us for our unbelief; yea, and he did preach unto us, much like our father, and he did tell us his version of the olive trees and grafting and the remnant of our seed; but behold, he did not know that we had left a remnant of our seeds

in Jerusalem to make room for the precious things we had smuggled into our packs, all of which was finally lost to that bounder Laban.

17 And behold, Nephi did explain the dreams of our father, and he did use terms like wickedness and filthiness a lot.

18 Now I, Laman, do not write all of the words of my brother, for most of them went in one ear and out the other; but behold, I did like my interpretation better, for it was not complicated and was less religious and much shorter.

19 Yea, the words of Nephi were hard, for we had been limping along in the wilderness and were tired and short tempered and could not bear to sit still for such a long-winded interpretation; yea, and we did not like to be reminded of our filthiness all the time, for we had done our best to keep clean in the river Laman, and this was just a camping trip anyway; wherefore, we could tidy up when we got home to Jerusalem again in about forty years.

20 Now behold, Nephi did admit that his words were hard, and he said that the truth was always hard unto the wicked, for it cutteth them to the very center.

21 And I, Laman, and also my brother Lemuel, did suspect that Nephi was speaking about us; but behold, I had never thought of myself as wicked, nor my brother Lemuel either— perverse, maybe, but not wicked.

22 Wherefore, we did feel hurt at the words of Nephi, and we did wish that he would be more like unto Sam, who said little; yea, Sam did not bellyache when we tied him up, nor complain when our father did not name anything after him, neither did he seem to have very many dreams.

CHAPTER 11

There are marriages galore in the wilderness—Lehi finds a brass ball to go with his brass plates, but it points in the wrong direction—The sons of Lehi go hunting without a license—Nephi breaks the only decent bow, and the murmuring goes right off the scale—The brass ball works by magic.

AND it came to pass that Zoram took the eldest daughter of Ishmael to wife, right there in the wilderness; yea, we were so busy interpreting dreams and delving into horticulture that we didn't notice that old Zoram was getting sheep eyes; wherefore, there was much rejoicing amongst us, for it was our custom that no one of a man's daughters could marry until the oldest was hitched, and Ishmaela—for that was the name of the oldest daughter—was getting a little long in the tooth. Now I did see the wisdom in bringing Zoram with us into the wilderness, for he was getting a tad wrinkly himself; yea, he pretty well took me, the oldest son, off the hook.

2 Now after Zoram was married, behold, the matrimonial floodgates did open, and we were awash in nuptials; yea, I did take to wife Morona, the most fetching daughter of Ishmael, and my brethren also

"And it came to pass, that Zoram took the eldest daughter of Ishmael to wife; yea, and I, Laman, was exceedingly relieved."

LAMAN 11:3-11

took of the daughters of Ishmael to wife; and even the exchange student had goo-goo eyes for one of my sisters and was caught up in the connubial bliss, and a cousin did latch onto the other sister; wherefore, the bonds of matrimony did encircle us in one great clove hitch.

3 Now, all these things were done as my father dwelt in a tent in the valley of Lemuel, and it was a good thing he slept and dreamed so much or you can bet they never would have happened.

4 And it came to pass that I did promise to take Morona back to Jerusalem for a honeymoon if she would wait for the next dream of my father, for I did expect to be sent packing on another errand, probably for a few more tents and a crib or two.

5 Now behold, she did not have to wait long; yea, we had scarcely finished with the freeze-dried wedding cake when my father had another dream; and behold, he commanded that we should again trudge off into the wilderness; wherefore, I had hopes that we would head north in our wanderings, now that winter was coming on; yea, I did wish that we might get back home for the holidays.

6 But as my father arose one morning and went forth from his tent, lo and behold, to his great astonishment, he found upon the ground a strange metal object lying in the sand, and he did call everybody together.

7 And behold, it was a round, brass ball with two spindles or needles, like unto a compass or astrolabe, and Nephi did handle it and did remark about its curious workmanship and fine brass, and I did wonder what careless Bedouin had left it lying before the tent of my father, and I did suspect that somebody besides us must be wandering lost in the wilderness.

8 And it came to pass that my father did look closely at the ball; and behold, he said that one of the needles pointed the way whither we should go into the wilderness, but behold, it did point in the wrong direction, for it was pointing farther away from Jerusalem; wherefore, I did ask my father to look at the other needle, for he was always bad with directions.

9 Now I, Laman, began to grumble again, and with good reason; for behold, we were rambling farther and farther from our home, which meant that when my father decided to send us back for something else he had forgotten to pack, it would become a major pilgrimage; yea, and Morona did have her heart set upon a little fun in the city, neither did we like being at the mercy of some curious device that pointed off into nowhere.

10 Now my father did call the brass ball the Liahona, which being interpreted means, and this is Lemuel's translation, Little Computer that Falls from Sky.

11 And it came to pass that we did gather together whatsoever things we could carry and packed our bags and departed again into the wilderness; yea, we did cross the river Laman and left the valley of Lemuel,

and I did never expect that I would be so sad to leave this place; but behold, we were about to stumble deeper into the wilderness, with nothing but the dreams of my father and a device of curious workmanship to give us goofball directions.

12 Now my wife, Morona, was exceedingly gloomy, for it did appear that we would not return again unto Jerusalem until the spring; yea, she did now refer to our honeymoon as a comedy of errors, but I did assure her that most honeymoons were like that.

13 And it came to pass that we did travel for the space of many days; and it was hot during the day and cold at night, and our feet grew sore and we were always hungry, for once my father got on the road, he did not like to stop.

14 And behold, by day I did curse the sand and wind and sun and groaned at the cold moon and stars by night; yea, to be carried away captive into Babylon did now seem more and more attractive, and I did often dream about it, and my brother Lemuel also.

15 And it came to pass that at last we did stop to rest from our wanderings, and we did pitch our tents in a place my father called Shazer, after the name of our near-sighted cousin. And I did feel sorry for Sam, that he did not have any place named after him; wherefore, I did comfort him by pointing out that this place was a dump, and that surely our father would find a nicer one later on, maybe a mountain that would be called after him, or perhaps some day even a club; yea, and I did console my brother, Nephi, that he should not feel hurt that he did not yet have landmarks named after him either, telling him that some day he might have a whole town or maybe even a bunch of people named after him.

16 And thus did I, Laman, speak comforting words unto my little brothers in the place of Shazer, where my father did pitch his tent for a mini-season.

17 And it came to pass that Nephi said that we should take our bows and our arrows and go forth into the hills to slay food for our families; but behold, I did remind him that we were in a strange land where it might not be hunting season, neither did we have a license; wherefore, he did remind me that such things had never bothered me before, and so I, Laman, did go off on the hunt.

18 Now behold, as my brothers went on ahead, I did stop to rest in a narrow draw covered with trees; and behold, a wild donkey did step forth from the thicket, neither did he see me sitting upon a cliff above him; wherefore, I did roll a large rock down upon him and did slay him.

19 And it came to pass that when my brothers returned empty-handed, behold, I had buried the head of the donkey and had skinned and quartered the beast so that it did look like a nice piece of venison; wherefore, we did return unto the tent of my father with meat for our families, neither did I bother to tell them that what they were

LAMAN 11:20-26

rejoicing over was a dead donkey; yea, and when Lemuel did later ask me what I had done with the head, I did explain that I had given it unto a passing nomad who wanted the horns for mounting.

20 Now behold, our stay in the place of Shazer was short, for we did again slosh off into the wilderness; yea, Sam was happy that the place had not been called after him, for we were there but three days, which annoyed our cousin, who said we might as well have given his name unto the moose I had shot.

21 And it came to pass that we did travel for the space of a few days, then camped for the space of a few more days, then hit the road again into the wilderness. Now behold, even with the Liahona it did seem that we were still merely wandering, for we did keep to the borders near the Red Sea without ever really going there, neither could we expect to catch any fish if we did, for our fishing rods were back at Jerusalem with the rest of our precious things.

22 Now it came to pass that we went forth to slay food nearly every day with our bows and our arrows and our slings; wherefore, we were always hungry, for we were lousy hunters; yea, most of us could not hit the broad side of a barn with a sling or an arrow, let alone a wild boar or a bounding deer; and behold, I would never have slain the wild donkey if it had not practically walked up to me and requested a hunter-assisted suicide.

23 Now behold, Nephi did hunt with a bow of fine steel, for he did always go first-class; wherefore, he did get most of the game, for Lemuel and Sam and I did all have cheap wooden bows that soon lost their zip; yea, I could hit nothing, not even a sick hyena, with my crummy bow; wherefore, I only went on the hunting trips because it was a man thing, and to get out of the tent.

24 And it came to pass that after many days of hiking and camping and hunting, behold, Nephi did break his nifty bow; wherefore, we did grow angry with him, for we had grown fond of eating almost every day; yea, without the steel bow of Nephi we were really behind the eight ball.

25 And we did return unto our families empty-handed and mournful, and they were tired from tramping around, and wandering made them exceedingly hungry; yea, they were sick of eating beans and turnips; wherefore, everyone got really moody and the children began to bawl and the adults began to murmur, and the murmuring became so loud that it frightened some of the camels and the horses; and behold, several of them up and bolted into the bush so that I, Laman, and also my brother, Lemuel, did have to go forth to look for them.

26 And it came to pass that after two days we did return with the animals that had nipped off; wherefore, everyone was sorry that they did murmur so loudly; yea, we did rebuke everybody, saying that in the future they should keep their murmuring

to an acceptable level or else next time they would have to go chasing after the spooked animals themselves.

27 Now behold, my wife, Morona, did complain unto me again, saying this was a really cheap honeymoon and that we should return at once unto Jerusalem or she would move back into the tent of her father, Ishmael; yea, she was sick and tired of prowling around the borders of the Red Sea and never once actually going there, especially since she had packed her Assyrian designer swim suit.

28 Yea, and even my father did murmur, which showed that he was finally coming to his senses; wherefore, I did propose that we stop this aimless wandering and hightail it back to Jerusalem and hustle over to the land of our inheritance before some squatters nabbed it; yea, I did recount unto our little party the whole nine yards of our sufferings and afflictions, saying that we might as well admit that our vacation just hadn't panned out; yea, and I did conjure up a picture of some of the best restaurants back home in Jerusalem and did recite unto them some of the menus by heart.

29 And now, as I was stirring the pot of passions and turning the thoughts of everyone unto Jerusalem and home, behold, Nephi was busy making another bow out of wood, and arrows from sticks, yea, we did point our fingers at him and mock him, which, remembering Lehi's dream, did seem like *deja vu* all over again.

30 And it came to pass that when Nephi had finished his new bow, he went straight unto our father, asking where he should go to obtain food; wherefore, I did provide the answer, shouting in a loud voice: Jerusalem! And behold, the entire company did crack up.

31 But Lehi did quietly retire unto his tent to inquire of the Lord; and behold, he came forth with the Liahona in his hands, and we did all look upon the ball and beheld new words written upon it, for it did have what looked to be a tiny monitor.

32 Now, I, Laman, do not write what we saw, but it did cause us to shake in our boots, for it was a kind of magic ball, and the things that did appear were the thoughts of our hearts, and each one saw his own, and we could not look upon it for long. And my father and my brother, Nephi, did gaze into the ball, neither did they say what they saw; but behold, it did show unto them the direction Nephi should go to hunt.

33 And it came to pass that Nephi went forth up onto the top of a mountain, and he did find wild beasts and did slay them with his bow and arrows; wherefore, he did again bring home the bacon, and we did rejoice and did no more guffaw at Nephi, neither did we doubt anymore the power of the ball or director which my father had found, but I, Laman, did not wish to look into it again, for it is terrible to look into the darkness of your own heart.

CHAPTER 12

Ishmael dies suddenly, which is

LAMAN 12:1-6

a lousy way to get out of wandering in the wilderness—His family begins to murmur in earnest, and Laman eggs them on, thinking it's time to take sides: patriside and fratriside—A voice tells Laman to watch his step, and it doesn't mean in the pasture.

AND it came to pass that we did again take our journey into the wilderness, traveling ever farther from our home, stopping from time to time to rest, then slugging along some more. And after the space of many days we did pitch our tents in a pathetic place which was called Nahom, and when I looked at it, I asked myself why anyone would want to live here, and wondered how they could make a living.

2 Now it came to pass that while we were camped at Nahom, Ishmael did complain of fatigue and light-headedness and other aches and pains, but then, hey, who didn't; yea, I wasn't exactly feeling chipper myself. But lo and behold, to our surprise, Ishmael dropped dead; wherefore, we were filled with sorrow, and I did inquire of Lemuel what in the dickens he died of, and Lemuel said he was just a hypochondriac; wherefore, he didn't die of anything.

3 Now the daughters of Ishmael did mourn exceedingly, and especially Morona, for she could no longer threaten to return unto the tent of her father when she was vexed with me; and behold, the family of Ishmael did murmur against my father who had brought them on this boring holiday, with stopovers in run-down, flea-bitten holes like Nahom, and here they would have to bury their father, neither could they travel all the way back to Nahom to put flowers on his grave on Memorial Day.

4 Now behold, I, Laman, was proud of the family of Ishmael, for I had taught them all they knew about murmuring, and I did remind them that Nephi was in cahoots with my father and that they should throw in a few murmurs about him; but behold, I did warn them that they should let me make sure the camels and horses were securely tied before the murmuring got too intense and we ended up with another stampede.

5 And I did speak secretly unto my brother Lemuel, and also unto the sons of Ishmael, saying: Behold, have we not wandered in the wilderness for so long that I have lost track of time, for my day planner was left back in Jerusalem with the other precious things; yea, and have we not followed the commands of Lehi, only to suffer much affliction and fatigue and sore feet and stiff joints and hemorrhoids from riding those miserable camels; and behold, are we not likely to end up horizontal like poor Ishmael; wherefore, were it not better to put the kibosh on Lehi, my father, yea, and on my brother Nephi, too, before they starved us to death or killed us with this vacation from hell?

6 Now behold, they did receive my speech with much approval, except that Lemuel did point out my mixed metaphor, saying that one cannot *end up* horizon-

tal; yea, and he did also remind me that there was the awkward problem of the Lord, who had spoken unto Lehi and also unto Nephi, and what about the alleged angels who had shown up from time to time.

7 But behold, I, Laman, did never let reality get in my way; wherefore, I did remind my brother that the Lord had spoken unto our father, Lehi, only in dreams, and that we were not present when angels ministered unto Nephi or our father, therefore, it should not count; yea, and Nephi was like unto Joseph of old, wanting to be a ruler and a teacher over his elder brethren, and maybe even hoping that there would be a musical written about him some day.

8 Now behold, one of the sons of Ishmael did bring up the business of the Liahona, for on it were written the words of the Lord for all to see, and it did direct us whither to go into the wilderness and it did help Nephi find good hunting in an area that wasn't even posted.

9 Now the Liahona did have me buffaloed, but then I was not brought up with computers; yea, I did suggest that Nephi did work many things by his cunning arts, for the hand is quicker than the eye; and behold, why would this voodoo ball point the way deeper into the wilderness where there is nothing but an occasional wide spot in the road like that rat trap Nahom?

10 And thus did I stir up the hearts of my brethren in anger against Nephi, and also against my father, Lehi; yea, now I did not wish only to turn tail and run back to Jerusalem, for it was not enuf for me to succeed; but behold, Nephi and my father had to fail; wherefore, I did plot to rub them out, for surely that would be their ultimate failure.

11 And it came to pass that as I patted myself upon the back for this diabolical plot, behold, a strange thing did happen, for we did all hear a voice, but we saw no man; yea, and the voice was like unto thunder, in that it did get our attention and did raise the hair on the back of my neck, yet it was not loud, but clear and certain, so that it did go right to the bone.

12 And behold, the voice did not sound very pleased with us, for it did chasten us for our iniquity, and it did reprove us for transgressing at least two of the ancient commandments given unto Moses, numbers five and six, I believe, and I did make a special note to look them up in the brass plates that my father kept in his tent, for I could never remember them in order, and some of them I had forgotten altogether.

13 And many other things did the voice speak unto us, which are too numerous to inscribe without getting writer's cramp, but I do remember that I was no more angry with my father or with my brother, Nephi, neither did I desire to bump them off; and behold, I was sorry that I had been so rotten on our trip; yea, it did seem that the hunger and thirst and afflictions, plus the daily threat of perishing in the wilderness—all added to the bad example of Lemuel—did bring out the worst in me;

LAMAN 12:14-14:5   36

wherefore, I did want to kick myself for being so despicable.

14 Now behold, Nephi did explain that the sound we had heard was the voice of the Lord, and I did almost believe him, for it did speak with great authority and we did know that it meant business.

15 And it came to pass that Nephi was pleased that we did not tie him up again or rub him out; wherefore, he did go off into the mountains and did slay more food for us, and we did not perish—yet.

CHAPTER 14

Years pass wandering—The game of golf is almost invented—Raw meat is added to the menu—They arrive in Bountiful, but Nephi grows weary of life on shore and decides to build a ship—The brothers grow angry with Nephi, with shocking results.

AND it came to pass that we did again take our journey into the wilderness, and we did leave the borders of the Red Sea and did travel eastward and did watch the seasons come and go; wherefore, we did observe the changes in the color of the endless sand, which Lemuel did describe as taupe and ecru and oatmeal and brindle and several other shades of brown that I had never heard of; yea, and it did seem that we were trudging clear across Arabia.

2 And it came to pass that our wandering stretched into months and then years, and our wives bore children in the wilderness, and our tents became exceedingly small; yea, our father Lehi did rejoice to count all of his seed, but then he did not have to sleep in the same tent with them; and behold, my wife did give birth unto our first-born son, and we did call him Moron, after his mother, Morona, and she did also give birth unto two daughters, Babylonia and Reebok, then two more sons, which we called Egad and Modicum; yea, our families began to grow until we did begin to look like unto a people, which is just slightly larger than a tribe.

3 And we did wade thru much affliction—yea, the operative word is wade, for if you have ever walked in sand or pitched a tent in sand or cooked your meals in sand or raised your children in sand, and done this day in and day out, then you will know what it means to wade thru affliction.

4 And life was very tedious; wherefore, we did entertain ourselves by placing a tiny ball in the sand and hitting it with a wooden club, which Lemuel did call a niblick, but there was no place to hit it, except back into more sand, which was no fun at all; wherefore, Lemuel did plant patches of grass that we might have little green spots beside the sand; yea, and we did hit the ball from one patch of green to another, trying always to keep the ball out of the sand; but lo and behold, rodents did bore holes in our grassy patches, and we did become discouraged when our balls rolled into the holes; wherefore, we did look for some other kind of diversion.

5 But behold, the coop de grass of our misery came when

The sons of Lehi did almost invent
the game of golf.

LAMAN 14:6-13

my father, Lehi, did announce that the Lord did prefer that we should not make much fire in the wilderness; wherefore, I did remind him that we were not in any danger of setting the place on fire, neither did we need to worry about burning down the dunes.

6 Now my father, Lehi, did always take a very rigid interpretation of the word of the Lord; yea, he did believe that we should no longer cook our meals but eat raw meat; and behold, he did say that the Lord would make our food to become sweet unto us, but it was never sweet unto me, only cold and raw and gaggy; wherefore, I did become a vegetarian.

7 And it came to pass that the years dragged by, and we did continue our wandering and wading; and behold, I did begin to suspect that our father, Lehi, was hoping to break the record for wandering held by the children of Israel; yea, and I did worry that our children would grow up thinking that life was just a beach.

8 And lo and behold, after what did seem an eternity, we did stumble upon the edge of a great sea, which my father named Irrigation, or something like that, which he said means many waters; yea, it was a whole magnitude of water, which I did expect since there had been so much beach leading up to it.

9 And behold, we pitched our tents in a verdant valley that looked out upon the sea, and our children did gather fruit from the many trees, and we found wild honey and much game; wherefore, my father called the place Bountiful, though we had no relative by that name; and behold, I did truly think it was the promised land; yea, I did sit against a tree and did look for hours upon the green land, while our children frolicked like young lambs and my eyes began to fill with tears, for I was sitting in a clump of stinging nettle.

10 Now after many days, I began to be exceedingly comfortable in the land of Bountiful, for we did have plenty to eat and a spectacular view with hardly any traffic; wherefore, my wife did make plans for a small bungalow near a fresh spring, thinking that we might fold up our borrowed tent for good.

11 But behold, Nephi did grow restless, for some people just don't know how to relax; yea, we did observe that he spent his time collecting skins of beasts, and with them he did make a strange contraption which he called a bellows wherewith to blow a fire, that he might make tools.

12 Now behold, I did gripe unto our father, Lehi, saying: If Nephi can build a fire to make his ball-peen hammer and his lug wrench, why could not we have a little fire for a barbecue? Yea, and why do we need tools in the first place, for have we not become hunters and gatherers, or are we now to become farmers, and will not this confuse those at BYU who will one day do a master's thesis on us?

13 But behold, all of our wandering had pretty well taken its toll on Lehi, and he did let Nephi run wild; yea, our broth-

er, who had been acting very strange, did one day drop a bombshell on us, saying: Behold, the voice of the Lord did come unto me and did tell me to construct a ship wherewith to carry us across these waters; and behold, I am making these tools that I might build the ship as the Lord directs me.

14 Now I, Laman, could not believe my ears, for Nephi did not know diddly squat about making boats, neither was I going to set foot in anything that he built, let alone take a trip across the sea and probably drop off the edge of the world in the process; yea, if the Lord wanted us to go sailing, why could he not provide the means, for he had caused the Liahona to be dropped from the sky at the door of the tent of my father, then why not just trot out the Faro's own ship, the *Queen Nefertiti*?

15 But behold, Nephi did insist that he could build a ship with the help of the Lord, but wouldn't you know it, he did ask for my help, and the help of Lemuel also, which shows that Nephi was a little off his rocker, for we didn't know beans about boats either.

16 And I, Laman, did point out a few flies in the ointment; namely, that if the Lord himself was planning to lend a hand, then we might as well go fishing, for if the Lord could create the whole world in eight or nine days, I forgot which, surely he could crank out a boat in the wink of an eye; yea, and many other clever and sarcastic things did I say unto Nephi.

17 And Lemuel did also wax witty, bugging Nephi to cough up the plans for this divine dinghy, for surely the Lord would not build a boat without a blueprint; yea, and we did all laugh at Nephi and tease him and call him a fool and a few other names that may be hard to translate.

18 And it came to pass that Nephi was much downcast, which did make us feel good, for there is nothing like the depression of others to cheer a body up.

19 But behold, after we had our fun, we did speak words of comfort unto Nephi, saying that we knew deep down that he did not really expect to build this new-fangled ark, and besides, the land Bountiful was a little short on gopher wood; yea, and Lemuel pointed out that there was no sign of rain in the forecast as in the days when old Enoch built his ark.

20 Wherefore, I said unto Nephi: Thou art like unto our father, Lehi, led away by the foolish imaginations of thy heart, or is it <u>thine</u> heart?

21 Yea, once we got warmed up, we did murmur for the umpteenth time about being dragged out of the land of our inheritance to wander in the wilderness and to wade knee-deep through afflictions and to toil through hot days and to gag on cold meals and to suffer the smell of camels, and never once in all these years visit Club Med.

22 And, of course, we did bring up the old chestnut about the people of Jerusalem being good and decent, for they did always seem much better from a distance; yea, and we did not omit

LAMAN 14:23-30

the part about the gold and silver and precious things that we had been forced to leave behind with that thug of a monkey's uncle, Laban.

23 Now behold, after our truly world-class murmuring, we did think that Nephi was ready to heave in the towel, and that he would no more pursue his foolish plans to fashion a frigate; but behold, we did ever underestimate the pigheadedness of our little brother; yea, he did again crank out the story of Moses and the children of Israel who were led out of bondage and fed mangos from heaven and were at last brought to a land of promise, which was all very interesting, but I did not see the connection.

24 Wherefore, I, Laman, did remark unto Nephi that we were not at all like the children of Israel, for we were not in bondage; yea, we had quit our promised land for this pitiful desert, neither had we seen any mangos growing along the way; and, behold, I did bet that the children of Israel could build fires any time they wanted to cook their meat or bake their mangos.

25 Now behold, Nephi did again rebuke me for my blindness, saying that there are more kinds of bondage than one; yea, he did recount the many blessings that we had received and did remind me about those infernal brass plates and did remind me of the angel we had seen, and the voice of the Lord we had heard, and many other things which had slipped my mind.

26 And it came to pass that we grew angry with Nephi, for there is nothing more annoying than for someone to point out your faults—especially things that you have no intention of correcting; wherefore, we did decide that it was show time; yea, maybe even lights-out time for Nephi, for as Lemuel said: It is easier to extinguish the light that illuminates your own darkness than to rekindle your light within.

27 Now it came to pass that we were about to seize Nephi and tie him up again; yea, we did conspire to give him a one-way baptism, when behold, he did stand forth and did tremble before us; yea, he did say that he was filled with the spirit, and if we touched him, we should wither even as a dried reed.

28 Now I, Laman, thought that this was a cheap trick; wherefore, I did command Lemuel to grab hold of Nephi, but he would not, neither would any of the cowardly sons of Ishmael.

29 And it came to pass that we did decide to let Nephi go this time; wherefore, he did continue to speak many unpleasant things unto us, neither did we touch him or lay our hands upon him, just to be safe; yea, and I did give considerable thought as to how we could shove him into the sea without actually touching him.

30 Now behold, after many days Nephi spake unto us, saying: Stretch forth thy hands and thou shalt not wither as a dried reed, but the Lord will shock you that you may know that he is the Lord and that he has instructed me to build a ship.

31 And I did push Lemuel forward, and he did reluctantly stretch forth his hand; and behold, he did not wither, which did cause him much relief, but he did jump about a foot into the air, for Nephi was fully charged; wherefore, we did all go forth, that we might also experience this new shock therapy; yea, we did each receive a few instructional volts straight from the hands of Nephi.

32 Now behold, we did now know that the Lord was with him and that we should no longer withhold our labor; yea, and because of this divine spark, we did name the ship in our brother's honor, calling it the *Arc of Nephi*.

CHAPTER 15

A ship of curious workmanship is built, but will it float?—Sailing beats wandering in the desert—Laman directs the on-board entertainment—Nephi tries to put the kibosh on the party, so they tie him up again—Laman becomes captain, but Lemuel doesn't know diddly about reading a compass.

AND it came to pass that Nephi did work the timbers with the tools he did fashion, neither would he allow us to do anything but grunt work; yea, he did go up into the mount oft to pray unto the Lord, and did return with new and weird ideas of what a ship should be; wherefore, we did labor long upon the ship, and behold, Lemuel did put a note in the suggestion box, requesting overtime pay for the flunkies.

2 Now behold, the ship did slowly take shape, and it was truly of curious workmanship, neither had we seen anything like unto it before, but then we did not see many ships in Jerusalem; and behold, Lemuel and I did carve out "Kilroy Was Here" on the side of the boat, just for fun.

3 And it came to pass that we did all agree that the craftsmanship was exceedingly fine; wherefore we did believe that the Lord must have been with Nephi, for when it came to construction, he was just as klutzy as the rest of us, yea, until now he couldn't tell a router from a crescent wrench.

4 And after the space of many days (too many, according to my brother Lemuel) the ship was complete, and my father spake unto us, saying that we should arise and go down into the ship, for he was as curious as we were to see if the thing would float.

5 Now behold, I, Laman, could kick myself, for I had watched Nephi build his curious boat and had even handed him the tools, but I did not believe that we would actually leave the land of Bountiful and cross the waters of Irrigation to go to who knows where; yea, it was always my hope that we would use the *Arc* for pleasure and maybe do some deep-sea fishing.

6 And it came to pass that sure enuf, Lehi spake unto us, saying that the voice of the Lord had spoken unto him, and that we should pile up the *Arc* with much fruit and meat and honey and seeds; yea, with all of the provisions that we had been

LAMAN 15:7-15

lugging around in no man's land for the last decade or two, and that on the morrow we should set forth to find the promised land.

7 Wherefore, I did remind my father that we had not yet made a test run, and that a vessel of curious workmanship may be all right to look at, for everyone did ooh and aah, but maybe we had better see if it kept out water!

8 But behold, my voice was not heard above the noise and excitement and chaos of our packing, for everyone was anxious to set sail, neither could I blame them, for the children had spent their entire lives mucking about in sand, and the rest were sick and tired of their wretched life on shore; wherefore, everyone was thrilled for a chance to go on a cruise.

9 And it came to pass that we did enter into the boat, everyone according to his age, with our wives and our children, for my father was always a stickler for order; but behold, I did think it would be prudent for me to board last, to make certain that we had not left anything important behind and to make sure that the fires at the bellows of Nephi were completely out.

10 But behold, to my surprise, the boat did not sink as I had feared, so I did hop aboard and did pull up the gangplank; yea, and we did sail away with shouting and much laughter, and I did lead the group in an old sea shanty I had picked up years ago in Joppa.

11 And lo, we did all like sailing, for the sea was calm and the ride was smooth, and it did beat the daylights out of bumping along on a smelly camel.

12 But on the third day the sea was no more calm, but began to heave and sway and cavort; wherefore, the children did think it was fun, and they did play in the spray of water and laugh at the wild rocking under our feet; but behold, I did grow exceedingly sick, so that I became well acquainted with the outermost rail of the boat, insomuch that I did wish I was back trudging thru the sand, for in the wilderness you could always climb off of the camel, but I could see no escape from this bouncing boat; yea, I did grow so wretched that I did even envy poor old Ishmael.

13 And it came to pass that after many days I did gain my sea legs and my stomach did right itself; wherefore, I did again feel like living and could visit the buffet once more; yea, I did grow right festive and did again become the life of the party; and behold, I did beg Lemuel that he should play upon his Jew's harp; wherefore, we did dance and sing and make ourselves exceedingly merry.

14 And I, Laman, did break out the wine that I had smuggled aboard, which I had won in a dice game with a drunken Bedouin, and before long we were feeling no pain; wherefore, I did sing a few bawdy songs that did bring down the house, and I did tell some very funny stories about the Phoenician's daughter.

15 And it came to pass that Nephi did not seem to enjoy our merriment, neither did he laugh at my jokes, for he could never

"And when the boat did begin to thrash about in the water, I did have a peek at the ball or compass myself; and behold, there were but four words that did appear."

LAMAN 15:16-22

accept alternative lifestyles; wherefore, I did suggest that he go to bed early, as did our father, Lehi, and not be a party pooper; yea, we did wish to kick up our heels, and behold, the ship was in good hands, for we could read the compass and steer the old bark perfectly well without him.

16 Now behold, I never did know anybody who worried so much about the Lord as Nephi; yea, he did think about the Lord continually and did wonder about what mood the Lord was in and how everything would appear unto the Lord and if he was getting enuf rest; but behold, I, Laman, did not lose any sleep worrying about the Lord, for I was always too busy with myself; wherefore, I did concentrate upon my own pleasure, for that did seem to me the whole purpose of life; yea, and cannot the Lord take care of himself?

17 But behold, when Nephi got hold of an idea, he did not let go of it; wherefore, he was like a dog on an old bone, neither would he be content to let us enjoy ourselves without bawling us out; yea, he did fear that the Lord would be angry with us for our rudeness, but I did remind him that it was he who was being rude by lousing up our fun; wherefore, I did suggest that he take Sam and go along to the game room for a little ping pong.

18 And it came to pass that the sons of Ishmael, who, I must say, could never hold their liquor, did grow rowdy and suggest that we should help Nephi to cool off; wherefore, we did pounce upon him and bind him, and we were about to hang him out over the back of the boat, but behold, Nephi did chastise us and tell us that we should use the word, astern, when referring to the rear of the boat, and that technically we were about to hang him aft.

19 Now our younger brother did always correct us; wherefore, we were chapped that he did try to rule over us with his superior knowledge, neither did we give two hoots about fore and aft or jibs and mizzen masts or anything else on a boat; and it came to pass, as we were about to dangle him in the waves as food for the fishes, behold, the ship did suddenly begin to thrash about in the water.

20 Yea, and I did give Lemuel a swift kick in the rear for not keeping the boat on course; but behold, he did not know what the course was, neither could he figure out the ball or compass; wherefore, I did have a look myself; and behold, there were but four words that did appear upon the Liahona: You Are Now Captain!

21 And I, Laman, was rather pleased; wherefore, I did fashion a new hat to wear, and I did make a large sign that said: The Captain's Word Is Law; and behold, I did give orders to everyone, and did learn some new words, like belay and avast and yo-heave-ho; yea, and I did point the boat in the direction of the promised land, or where I thought the promised land should be.

22 Now behold, a great storm arose, and we did almost tip over; wherefore, I did command my crew to show a leg and hop

to and do something, but they were a bunch of incompetents and were good for nothing but shuffleboard; and behold, the waves began to crash in upon our boat and we were soaked to the skin, and the boat rolled from one side to the other like a log; wherefore, my father, Lehi, said that we should unbind the cords that held Nephi, but I did remind him that I was the captain and that Nephi was not even an officer and could just stay down in steerage.

23 Then I, Laman, did go secretly unto Nephi and did inquire of him what I, the captain, should do; and behold, he did advise me to pray.

24 Now behold, that was not the answer I wanted, for the waves began to look like unto mountains and the winds whipped the sails so that we were driven upon the waters for the space of three days, or maybe it was four, and we began to fear exceedingly that we should all be drowned in the sea; yea, I began to be sorry that I was the captain, for I did not wish to go down with the ship.

25 Wherefore, I did change my mind and did think that perhaps Nephi should receive a field commission; yea, I did loose the bands that held him and did turn over to him my captain's hat and baton while I did go to look for a life preserver.

26 Now behold, Nephi did have the luck of the Irish, for as soon as I did unbind him and did give him my special hat, behold, the storm did cease and the compass did begin to work again; wherefore, it was easy as pie to get back on course.

27 Now behold, I could not believe his streak of good luck; yea, if Nephi fell into the sea he would climb out with his pockets full of fish. Now I, Laman, was certain that I was jinxed, and I knew that if I ever found a promised land, behold, it would be promised to somebody else.

CHAPTER 16

Laman cannot believe the sea is so large—They take up fishing to pass the time—Ahoy, the promised land—Nephi and Sam take to farming—Laman and Lemuel become environmentalists and dabble in metallurgy—Laman harbors some doubts about the stories of Nephi—Isaiah gives him a headache.

AND it came to pass that we did sail for many days, and I was amazed that there was so much water in the sea; yea, there was water everywhere, but not a drop to drink, for sea water tasted wretched; wherefore, we were glad that Nephi did force us to haul barrels and barrels of sparkling spring water on board before we set out.

2 Now behold, Lemuel did wonder why we did not meet any other boats, either whaling boats or the coast guard or maybe some other crazy cruisers; and behold, I did begin to bite my nails, for I was worried stiff that we were too far from shore and might even fall off the edge of the world.

3 But Nephi spake unto us, saying that the earth was round like unto a ball and that we would not drop off the edge be-

LAMAN 16:4-11

cause it had no edge; yea, we were safe in the hands of the Lord; but behold, I, Laman, could not see why we could not fall off of a ball, especially one that was slippery with water; yea, once, when we were hunting, I stepped on a ball-shaped rock and fell off and nearly broke my neck, so go figure; and behold, we had been in the hands of the Lord since the beginning, and look at poor Ishmael back in Nahom six feet under.

4 And it came to pass that I, Laman, and also my brother Lemuel, did take up fishing to pass the time and to take our minds off falling; yea, we did make long poles from our supply of bamboo, and we did attach to them lines like unto nylon, and at the end we did tie lures that we did fashion from earrings we had pinched from our wives when they were not looking.

5 And behold, we did borrow some of the tools of Nephi, when he was busy with the brass plates, and we did make hooks of metal and did cover them with thread and wool and feathers, that they might resemble various hatches, and we did become expert in all the arts of fishing, and we did spend endless hours, so that our wives did complain exceedingly.

6 But behold, we did ignore the nagging of our wives, for there was nothing in the pre-nuptial agreements against fishing; yea, and I, Laman, did make a large flag and upon it did write the words: I Fish, Therefore I Am, and did fly it off the back of the boat, and thus did we pass the days at sea, hooking some dandies and losing a few bigger ones; yea, we did add some tasty fish, like salmon and ruffie, to our crummy diet.

7 And it came to pass that after many days (way too many, as Lemuel said), behold, one of the children did yell: Land ahoy! And we all looked, and sure enough, there was a sliver of land peeking over the rim of the sea.

8 And it came to pass that my father, Lehi, did call it the promised land; but behold, I would have settled for just about any old land, for I had grown weary of life at sea; yea, I did not wish to set foot on a boat ever again, neither did I ever want to go down to the sea again, to the lonely sea and the sky.

9 Now behold, the promised land was a huge improvement over our boat: for one thing, it did not move; and for another, it was lots bigger, neither did we find any sand, as in our last wilderness, except upon the beach where it belonged; yea, this was a new kind of wilderness, for it was covered with trees and forests and even a jungle or two, according to Sam, who must have looked it up in his atlas.

10 And behold, there were fresh streams and rivers, and we did find food in abundance, and there were animals of all kinds, although Lemuel did insist that I was exaggerating, for he did not remember seeing any giraffes or elephants or several other species like he had once seen at a zoo in Babylon.

11 And we did discover all manner of ore, including gold

and silver and other precious metals; wherefore, I did think that we had died and gone to heaven, or at least back to Jerusalem.

12 Now it came to pass that my father, Lehi, did instruct us to till the land and to plant the seeds that some of the others had brought; yea, most of my seeds were left behind in Jerusalem, and Lemuel did secretly dispose of nearly all of his seeds as we wobbled around in no man's land.

13 Now behold, Nephi, and also Sam, did seem to enjoy grubbing about in the soil and trying to coax seeds to grow, but I did not care much for farming, nor did my brother Lemuel, for we were constantly clearing the land and hauling rocks and removing stumps, and all by hand, for we had neglected to bring a tractor; yea, and I did wonder why we should come to a promised land that was covered with beautiful trees, then cut them down to plant corn; wherefore, Lemuel and I did try to protect the rain forests.

14 And so I, Laman, and my brother Lemuel did spend the better part of our time scrounging for gold and silver and other valuables, for we had a lot of catching up to do, since we had lost everything but our shirts to that meatball Laban.

15 And behold, I did design beautiful head bands and bracelets of silver and did create decorations and fishing lures of bright copper; yea, and Lemuel did fashion an exquisite small gold earring which he did wear until our father, Lehi, made him take it out.

16 And we did become a prosperous and numerous people, for our wives did have many children; yea, even my mother did continue to bear children, for, as Lemuel said, our father did have frost upon the chimney, but kept the fire going in the hearth.

17 Now behold, I said I would never again mention the brass plates of Laban; yea, I did wish they were the brass plates of somebody else, for just the name of that miserable hound did cause me to break out in hives, and the ordeal of fetching those plates, and losing all of our gold and silver and you-know-what, is still fresh in my mind; nevertheless, I must write somewhat of the words of Nephi, for he did read the brass plates constantly, when he wasn't farming, and he did speak about the things written upon them as if they were real and happened yesterday; yea, he did take it upon himself to be our teacher.

18 Now I do not write all that Nephi spoke, for he did speak much, and most of it I slept through; but behold, he did tell one story that was so hard to swallow that I must write it down.

19 Now behold, Nephi did declare unto us that God himself should come to earth as a man in six or seven hundred years, I do not remember which; yea, and that he should live among men, more or less in disguise, doing good, healing the sick, making the lame to walk, and even raising the dead to life, which is a service that poor Ish-

mael could have used, tho I would have hated to see it employed in the case of Laban.

20 And behold, the people would take this God who walked among them, helping them out of trouble and feeding the hungry and healing the sick and shoveling out good advice and in general being a decent sort of God; yea, and the people would arrest him and frame him at a phony trial and then nail him to a cross, as the prophet Zenock said, and crucify him, according to the words of the prophet Neum.

21 Now I, Laman, couldn't believe such a stretcher, for how could anybody be that muttonheaded, and why would people cut off their noses to spite their faces; yea, and why would folks wish to kill someone, whether he was a God or not, who stumped among them as their servant, dishing out the best pills for what ailed them, and doing all sorts of fancy miracles and especially not asking them to wander off into some wilderness; and besides, let's face it, you can't kill God; yea, it would be stupid to even try.

22 And behold, Nephi did agree, for he did say that this God would remain in a tomb of darkness for the space of about three weeks, I believe it was, and afterwards, as the prophet Zenos says, he should come back to life again; yea, he should even take time out from his busy schedule and make a brief appearance unto our seed.

23 Now I, Laman, do not care a fig about the past, nor do I give a hang about Zenos and Zenock and Neum or any of the other prophets I have never heard about before, except that Nephi scrounged them up from the plates of brass, neither do I see how anyone can predict the future; yea, especially the future that tells such a whopper about God coming to earth and then a bunch of idiots trying to bump him off.

24 Yea, the big problem with prophecies and miracles and signs is that they always happen somewhere else and to somebody else and in some other dispensation; wherefore the whole system is impossible to check up on.

25 Now behold, Nephi did remind me that I myself had seen miracles and signs, and that they were not just in the past or in the future; yea, I had been visited by angels, tho I did remind him that the singular would be more appropriate, because I did remember only one; and behold, he said that I had also heard the voice of the Lord, and I had held the Liahona in my own hands, and I had read the words of the Lord that did appear mysteriously upon it.

26 And I did have to admit that all of these things did happen unto me, but that they did seem less miracle-like somehow, maybe because they were so close to home and not in some book, like in the brass plates of that ninny Laban.

27 And behold, I did tell Nephi that these fresh miracles might be explained away; to wit: could not the angel in the cave have been just a spy for that wretched and now defunct Laban, and might not the voice of the Lord have been merely an-

other of Nephi's ventriloquist tricks? yea, and as Lemuel said: How do we know that the ball of curious workmanship was not sold unto our gullible father by some pushy reformed Egyptian who downloaded onto it some of the sorcery devised by that famous magician of Faro, David Potterfield by name?

28 Then Nephi did speak unto me, saying: All miracles and signs can be explained away, for there is no miracle or sign that will convince a wicked man, except his heart be changed.

29 But behold, I, Laman, could still not swallow Nephi's story, for if God were to wander among us and conjure up a mess of miracles and heave out a bunch of signs, what nincompoop would deny it, and what fat head would want to break himself off and bring down upon him a whole heap of wrath?

30 And so Nephi did try to pound into our skulls some of these far-fetched teachings from the brass plates; yea, just because he liked genealogy and could read well, he did set himself up as a teacher and ruler over us; and behold, Nephi did know how to hit where it hurts, for he did trot out the words of Isaiah from time to time, saying that his soul did delight in the words of Isaiah, and this he did knowing that the words of Isaiah were just gibberish unto us; yea, I did read all of chapter forty-eight once and did not get one thing out of it except a headache.

31 Now behold, Nephi did continue to annoy us by reciting this mumbo jumbo and pretending to know what it meant; yea, it was like rubbing salt in our wounds, and we were sick and tired of so much salt; therefore, Lemuel and I did secretly plot for some way to send Nephi off to glory, perhaps for a private reunion with old Isaiah himself.

CHAPTER 17

Laman gives an account of his tin plates—The promised land is not a bed of roses—Lehi gives the older boys a scolding, then grows old.

NOW I, Laman, write somewhat concerning these plates of tin whereupon I do keep this account; yea, I did make them with mine own hands, with a little help from my brother Lemuel, for he became a semi-skilled worker in all branches of metallurgy, and he did work with copper and nickel and zinc and titanium, yea, he did enjoy dabbling in all of the elemental metals. And his own small plates, which I hope to high heaven you never have to read, upon which he gives his own warped account of our trials and tribulations and many afflictions, were cast from lead.

2 And behold, I did warn Lemuel that lead was not a good choice, for a record of more than a few pages would require a forklift to transport, and who knows when we might be commanded to pack up, lock, stock, and barrel, including all of our plates, and hit the road again, or maybe even sail the seven seas; but behold, he did insist that his plates of lead were soft and easy to inscribe upon, yea,

"Now behold, we did find all manner of useful beasts in the forests, and, as Lemuel said, we did also find a good many that were totally useless." (17:9)

their excessive weight would compel him to be brief; wherefore, I did concede the wisdom of his choice, knowing well his literary gifts.

3 And it came to pass that I did learn from my son, Moron, who was sent to keep an eye upon Nephi, that my little brother had pounded out some plates of gold, upon which he did write an account of our wanderings and seafarings and promised landings; yea, Moron did report that Nephi had made both big gold plates and small gold plates, wherefore I did suppose that he was using the double entry method.

4 Now behold, when I learned of the plates of Nephi, I did go at once to Lemuel with a plan to hammer out some plates of my own whereupon I could inscribe a true and impartial account of these same events; yea, I could tell my own story without a lot of religion and prophecies and scriptures, especially Isaiah.

5 Now behold, these tin plates were harder to make than you would think, for we were starting from scratch and had no recipe, neither did I check with Nephi as to the optimum size for historical plates; wherefore, our first tin plates were large sheets roughly four feet by eight feet, which I did think was a little too cumbersome and almost as bad as *The Little Plates of Lemuel,* which weighed in at about 400 lbs.

6 But Lemuel did devise a way to bend the tin into rippled sheets just two feet by eight feet; yea, after I had inscribed our history upon one sheet, behold, it did serve as a perfect covering for the little bungalow that Morona had forced me to build, and the tin plates did keep out the water much better than sod or banana leaves; wherefore, she did nag me until I had to write day and night that our roof would be complete before the fall hurricane season.

7 Now it came to pass that life in the promised land was not all peaches and cream, for there were many insects and spiders and bugs and other nasty creatures that we had never seen in our forced march across Arabia, neither could we find them in any of Sam's entomology books; yea, some of them were exceedingly large and vicious, and they did bite with a vengeance, and we were constantly swatting and hitting at them so that the tranquillity of the promised land was punctuated by the sound of flesh smacking flesh; wherefore, I did complain that we had brought way too many seeds and nobody had remembered to pack the mosquito netting or the bug bomb.

8 And there were snakes; yea, the jungles were just chock full of snakes; and behold, I did never like snakes, and I did wonder why we could not be led unto a promised land like Ireland.

9 Now behold, we did find all manner of useful beasts in the forests and in the jungles, and, as Lemuel said, we did also find a good many that were totally useless, but behold, I was surprised to see cattle and horses and sheep; wherefore, I did worry that we had not been given top billing and that we

LAMAN 17:10-16

were not the first to be led to this promised land, and I did wonder if we were just renting or if we had the deed; yea, Lemuel did have nightmares wondering why the last tenants had decided to pack their bags and leave.

10 Now the useful beasts in the forest were no longer tame; wherefore, to call them useful was a misnomer, for they were not worth a plug nickel until we corralled them, for they had become as wild as a March hare; yea, and we did have a devil of a time trying to catch them, for we were on foot and were outnumbered in that category by two to one.

11 And behold, one day as we went out on a roundup, I did hook a rope on a wild cow, and she did drag me through the brush and across a field for half a mile before Lemuel did stop her; yea, and Lemuel did chew me out for not letting go of the rope, but I did explain that I couldn't let go, for it was wrapped around my wrist; wherefore, I was sore and cut and bruised and mad, neither did I wish to tame that cow, for I would not be content until she was carved into hamburger.

12 And it came to pass that we did scour the wilderness and search the forests for months until we had rounded up a few paltry horses and punched us a small herd of cows; yea, we did have fresh milk and cheese and butter; but after a few weeks of milking night and morning, even on weekends and holidays, I did complain unto Lemuel, saying that it was miserable being a farmer, but it was hell being a dairyman.

13 And it came to pass that one day as I was murmuring about the beastly chores and complaining about the blasted bovines, behold, my father, Lehi, did overhear me, and he did call me unto him, and he did summon my brother, Lemuel, and the sons of Ishmael also; yea, he did call pretty much all of the sons together, and I did suspect that we were in for another good tongue-lashing.

14 Now behold, my father was becoming absent-minded, and he did sometimes call me Lemuel and did occasionally wear socks that did not match, but he did not forget any of our old blunders; yea, he did retain a keen remembrance of all of our wickedness; wherefore, he did recite the whole concatenation of our offenses, beginning from the time we left Jerusalem unto the present, with particular mention of our behavior aboard that wretched ship, as well as the excessive number of times we had tied Nephi up, though he was off by two since a couple of our rope therapy sessions, as Lemuel called them, had taken place in the privacy of the desert.

15 And behold, our father did remind us that this land was a choice land; yea, it was head and shoulders above all other lands, and that none should be brought unto this land save it be by the hand of the Lord.

16 And I, Laman, did hope that with the next batch of chosen people the Lord would use a kinder and gentler hand than he did with us, and maybe

LAMAN 17:17-25

chuck out the wandering in the desert part; yea, it did seem to me that nobody would volunteer to be the chosen people any more if they knew that part of the bargain was to slog around for years in the wilderness and maybe get killed off in the process, and then not get a clear title to the promised land when they got there!

17 And it came to pass that as my father, Lehi, spake unto us about the amenities of our new real estate, behold, he did drop another grenade, for he did tell us that he had seen in a vision that Jerusalem had finally been destroyed; yea, we would also have perished if the Lord had not been merciful unto us and warned us that we should flee.

18 But behold, he said nothing about the old Babylonians, and I did wonder if our good friends might not be having more fun in Babylon than we were here in Timbuktoo.

19 And I was glad that I did not see the fall of dear old Jerusalem in any vision, for I did want to remember it as I had always known it; yea, I, Laman, and my brother Lemuel also, did like to believe that we had brought a little bit of Jerusalem with us into the promised land.

20 And it came to pass that as my father, Lehi, spake unto us, he did appear old and tired and worn out; and I, Laman, had not noticed this before, for he had always been just a father unto me, and I had never looked upon him as someone who would not always be there to lecture me and to shout at me and to sometimes thwack me, as he had been forced to do many times while I was growing up, but that he could waste away and wither like the leaves and fade and die like all other living things.

21 Yea, and he began to weep, saying that he must soon lie down in the cold and silent grave and return unto the dust of the earth, and he did admonish us to awake from the sleep of hell and shake off the chains with which we were bound; yea, he did mourn for us because of our iniquity.

22 And I, Laman, did look upon my father with different eyes, for they were now a little misty, and for the first time in my life I saw a father who truly loved his sons and whose heart was weighed down with sorrow because he feared that at least two of them would be lost forever, and I don't mean Nephi and Sam.

23 And I beheld an old and gentle and good man who was dying in a strange land, far from his home; yea, he had given up everything, and his gold and his silver and his precious things were now his family and his faith in God; wherefore he did believe that God had been good and merciful unto him and had brought him into a promised land that would be a legacy unto his seed forever.

24 Yea, and he had suffered hardships and afflictions and hunger and thirst; and behold, he had even thanked God for doing all these things unto him, and he did consider himself the happiest of men.

25 And it came to pass that after my father had spoken unto us, I did go off by myself into

Prototype of the Plates of Laman before Lemuel
suggested the use of tin.

the forest, and I did sit and think; yea, and all of my wickedness and abominations did come into my mind; wherefore I did sit and think for many hours, and my heart was filled with sorrow that I had been such a lousy son, and I did see that my brother Lemuel had been a bad influence upon me, and I was sorry that I did hang out with so many non-member friends; yea, I did regret that I had not been the baby of the family, for then maybe I would have been the righteous and good son instead of the odious older brother.

26 And behold, I did find myself so loathsome that I was about to throw myself into the river, until I did recall that I could not swim.

CHAPTER 18

Lehi blesses his children, but Laman gets a left-handed blessing—Laman expounds upon the teachings of his father—Lehi dies; wherefore, the moratorium on tying up Nephi comes to an end.

AND it came to pass that when I returned from the forest, behold, I did promise myself that I would turn over a new leaf; wherefore, I would pay attention when my father spake unto us about his many dreams; yea, and I would start each day by reading from the brass plates of Laban, except from Isaiah, and I would save every Monday night for family home evening and not go shopping on the sabbath, and give up fishing on Sunday, at least during the winter.

2 Now behold, my father, Lehi, did call all of his sons together again, but this time he did wish to give unto them a blessing; and behold, he did give exceedingly long blessings unto Nephi and unto Jacob and Joseph, his two sons born to him as surprises during our sand period, as we called it; but unto me and unto my children he did give a very short blessing; yea, it was a sort of left-handed blessing, for he did bless my children that any cursing that may come upon them would be answered upon the heads of their parents, and I did not like the sound of that, for it did seem a little negative; wherefore, I did wonder if my children might not take advantage of it, knowing that any curses upon them would not count, and they would get off scot-free; yea, I had always tried to teach my children to take individual responsibility for their curses.

3 And my father did call Lemuel and his family together, saying: Behold, I leave unto you the same blessing which I left unto Laman and his family; wherefore, Lemuel did mark Lehi down with a ten for brevity, but only one for originality.

4 And Lehi did call all the sons of Ishmael and their families together and did give unto them a blessing, which I do not write down because they should keep their own records and make their own plates and not have me or Aunt Hazel or anybody else doing their genealogy for them; and Lehi did also call Zoram and his family for a blessing, and he did call the exchange student and my sisters

and cousins and their families together and did give them a blessing; yea, and Lehi was all blessinged out and was ready to return unto his tent, when behold, a little child did stand up and shout, saying: What about Sam?

5 Wherefore, my father did remember Sam and did call him and his family together, and he did give unto him a very brief blessing, more or less lumping his seed with the seed of Nephi, which seemed fine with Sam, who was always easy-going and good-natured and quiet.

6 Now I, Laman, write somewhat concerning the teachings of my father, Lehi, for he did instruct us much about our first parents and the fall of Adam and the forbidden fruit, and he did prime us about foreordination and free agency and oppositions and prepositions and the direct objects of life; wherefore, I do set down these lessons as part of my homework; yea, I will inscribe what I still remember, for I have already forgotten most of the things my father said, since he did quote a lot of scriptures and did put us thru the mill, and if I leave anything out, you might check out the brass plates, or you could look it up in the big or little gold plates of my younger brother.

7 And it came to pass that our first parents were called Adam and Eve, and they were made by the Lord from the sand of the earth, which made perfect sense since the Lord seemed to hang out around the Holy Land a lot where there was no shortage of raw materials.

8 Now behold, I did ask my father if this were merely figurative, for I did think it were more likely that our first parents did evolve from lower life forms stretching clear back to the primordial slime, while Lemuel did discount my theory and did conjecture that the first man and woman were brought here from some other galaxy and transplanted, for on more than one occasion during our migration Lemuel did see things in the sky that could not be explained, which did give credence to the whole idea of UFOs.

9 But my father, Lehi, did not want to delve into these mysteries, saying only that God created them and placed them to live in the Garden of Eden, where they did enjoy a life of comfort and ease; wherefore, I knew right away that Adam and Eve were in trouble, for the Lord does not let anyone get too comfortable when they might just as well be off somewhere wandering or sacrificing a burnt offering.

10 But at first the Lord did pretty much leave Adam and Eve alone, saying that they had the run of the place, with no rent, if they would only keep the garden spruced up and preserve the peace and make sure the lion did lie down with the lamb and not start licking his chops.

11 Now behold, there was one other kicker, for there was a tree in the Garden of Eden that bore a forbidden fruit, and Adam and Eve could not partake of the fruit of that tree because it would kill them; wherefore, I did suspect that it was a kumquat,

for I did once eat some green kumquats and did become exceedingly sick and did almost die myself.

12 And it came to pass that life in the Garden of Eden was soft, but it was not all clover, for there were snakes; yea, and one of the most devious and wretched varieties was called Loosifer. Now behold—and I did not quite understand this part—it seems that this was some sort of talking snake; wherefore, he was even worse than a regular snake; but behold, Lemuel did insist that it was a metaphorical snake; yea, I figure that he was a sort of slimy person like unto that snake-in-the-grass Laban.

13 Now behold, this Loosifer did snooker Adam and Eve into eating one of the kumquats, for he did lie thru his teeth, telling them that it was delicious to the taste and that they would not surely die, which was half true; yea, he did say that the fruit would actually make them wise, knowing good from evil, which was true; wherefore, they did eat.

14 And behold, they did become wise in a hurry, and I did know exactly how they did feel, for if they did not die at once, they did feel like they had one foot in the door; yea it does show the wisdom of the Lord, for a green kumquat is the fastest way I know of to distinguish good from evil.

15 Now behold, the Lord did not think that Adam and Eve had suffered enough by partaking of this wretched fruit; wherefore, he did cancel their lease on the garden and sent them off to till the earth and to become farmers; and behold, here we do see the mercy of the Lord, for he could just as well have made them set up a dairy.

16 Now my father, Lehi, did say that this was what people called the fall of man, but he did teach us that it was more of a stumble than a fall, for if Adam and Eve had remained in the Garden of Eden and kept their hands off the kumquats, behold, they would have had no children; wherefore, they would have remained in a state of innocence, having no joy, for they knew no misery.

17 And I, Laman, having had many children, do understand exactly what my father did mean, for there is nothing like children to take away your innocence; yea, when the twins were born, Dan and Beersheba, we did have our innocence totally shattered, and when our oldest son, Moron, became a teenager, I did come face to face with the fall of man.

18 Now my father, Lehi, did teach us many other things, some of which I have inscribed in my private diary, for he did pepper his prophecies and sermons with graphic allusions, for he did speak of the seed of his loins and the fruit of our loins and the gentiles, and many other such things; wherefore, I did not think they should be recorded on these plates where the children might read about them.

19 And it came to pass that my father, Lehi, did finish his blessings and his teachings and his prophesying and did lay down the brass plates for the

last time.

20 And it did come to pass that Lehi died and was buried in his promised land, and we did mourn for him, for he was a good and righteous man; and behold, I was sorry that I had waited so long to become a righteous son, and I did hope that my seven days of holy-mindedness before he died were a comfort unto him; yea, for a whole week I did not murmur or tie up Nephi.

21 And not many days after the death of Lehi, behold, Nephi was again constrained to speak unto us and to give us some admonitions of the Lord; yea, I have never seen a person constrained as often as Nephi, for at the drop of a hat he could get almost blue in the face with constraining.

22 Now, upon the death of Lehi, behold, I, Laman, was the eldest, not counting Zoram and his wife Ishmaela; wherefore, I did believe that it was only right that I should become the big kahoona, neither did I think that Nephi should get top billing just because he happened to be more righteous or because he could work the Liahona.

23 And behold, I did persuade my brother Lemuel, and also the sons of Ishmael, that we should tie up Nephi again; yea, Lemuel did agree that it was about time to take Nephi for a ride; wherefore, I did run straight out and try to catch the horses, but Lemuel did call me back, telling me not to take everything so literally.

CHAPTER 19

Nephi is afflicted with the wandering disorder and goes off into the wilderness again, taking many others with him—Laman sets himself up as the big kahoona.

AND it came to pass that one morning as I awoke from my sleep, having been out fishing late, and it being about the ninth hour (now we did number the morning hours from one to ten, beginning at midnight, and the evening from one to ten, beginning at midday, and this we did to please Sam, who concocted this time-keeping method, being partial to the metric system), and behold, one of my children, little Agonia, did ask me where all of the people had gone.

2 Now, I did peer out of my bungalow, and, lo and behold, many of the horses and much of the cattle and all of the tents were gone; yea, half of the tribe had skipped off and were A.W.O.L.

3 And behold, I did rush over to roust out my brother Lemuel, and we did hustle over to the boat and found it safe and sound; wherefore, we did search the compound and did find nothing of Nephi and his family, nor of Sam and his family, nor of Zoram and his family, neither my sisters and their families, for they had all packed up, lock, stock, and brass plates, and gone off into the wilderness; yea, and our mother was gone, too.

4 Now I, Laman, did see that once a person has been led into the wilderness by the Lord, it is almost impossible to get the wanderlust out of his system;

yea, when the Lord finds somebody who is restless and can't settle down and actually likes the open road, He must be in seventh heaven.

5 And it came to pass that my first reaction was to say: Good riddance to bad rubbish, but then we did decide to take an inventory, that we might see what the deserters had pinched from us; and behold, they had left us half of the seed and half of the cattle and also a few horses and sheep that Lemuel had caught and tamed, plus a bunch of rusty tools that I had borrowed from Nephi and left out in the rain.

6 And behold, the brass plates were finally gone, and I was happy to be rid of them, for they had caused us constant grief from day one, and I was fed up to here with genealogy; yea, I was sick and tired of hearing all of those old prophesies and of trying to figure out the words of Isaiah when I didn't even have a secret decoder ring.

7 And Nephi did also carry off the ball or director, which I was sorry to lose because Morona thought it would look nice on the mantel, if I ever got around to building one; but behold, since I could not operate the darn thing anyway, we did console ourselves by thinking that it would have been just one more thing to dust.

8 But what did chap me was that they had purloined the sword of Laban, and I did want that sword in the worst way, for in the nice little weapons collection I had started, that would have been the trophy piece; yea, I was convinced that it was worth a bundle!

9 And it came to pass that we did give a name unto this mad urge to go off into the wilderness; yea, we did call it the wandering disorder, and Lemuel did insist that it was an hereditary problem, for my father was a descendant of Abraham, who wandered to all sorts of exotic places, with names like Ur of Chaldees and Gotham and Samorra; and behold, Joseph of old was also in our direct line; yea, he was so sorely afflicted that he got himself sold to some wandering Jaredites, I believe it was, just so he might slip on down and take a gander at Egypt; yea, and I think that Moses was also our relative, although I do not have the brass plates any more to check this out, but he had a very bad case of the wandering disorder, for he gad about in the wilderness for about 400 years, as I recall.

10 Now it was clear that my father, Lehi, did inherit a healthy dose of the genes that caused this wandering disorder, for although he did not wander the longest, he did set the record for distance, and he did get extra credit for wandering in a mixed media, both sand and water.

11 Now behold, Nephi did become the heir presumptive to this disease; wherefore, it was no great shock to see him creep off again, taking a whole passel of people with him, for almost everybody who gets sick and lights out into some wilderness or other prefers to have a lot of company to share in the misery; yea, as Lemuel did say: Nobody likes to wade thru afflictions

alone.

12 And it came to pass that I, Laman, did puzzle over their sudden departure, for it was just a few weeks before Christmas, and I did think that everyone was like me and hated to travel on holidays; but behold, Lemuel did scold me, saying that I had tied up Nephi one time too many.

13 And it came to pass that I did feel hurt that Nephi and Sam and little Jacob and Joseph and old Zoram and all their families had wandered off into the wilderness because of me; for behold, I did always believe that our little differences were only conventional sibling rivalry; yea, I did think of my murmuring and complaining and tying Nephi up as a normal response of an older brother who was repeatedly challenged by an over-achieving younger brother.

14 Now behold, I could not believe that Nephi would take our mother and all of the others with him, or that he would abandon the promised land; but Lemuel did remark that maybe the promised land was a bigger piece of real estate than we had thought; yea, it might include property on both sides of the narrow neck of land.

15 And it came to pass that I, Laman, did take the bull by the horns; wherefore, I did call the residue of the people together, and they consisted of my family and the family of Lemuel and the families of the sons of Ishmael and the family of the exchange student; yea, I did think it was high time for a powwow with the remaining homesteaders in this center stake of Zion.

16 Now behold, I did speak unto them on this wise, saying that following the death of my father, Lehi, behold, it had fallen upon me, the eldest son, to be the head honcho, and I knew that none of them wanted such a big responsibility, for it was lonely at the top, but somebody had to do it; yea, Nephi did try to muscle in on the job, for he had always wanted to be first fiddle, and I might have let him try his hand at it once he was properly trained, but now he had wandered away and was out of the running.

17 And I did explain unto them that if I did all of the work of ruling over them and did bear all of the heavy burdens as their boss, behold, they should promise to be my people and I would agree to be their king; yea, they must do all of the things that I did tell them to do; and behold, if they did not like it, they could lump it, for this was no democracy, neither would there be one in the promised land until long after the pilgrims.

18 And I did suggest unto them that they should henceforth be called Lamanoids, after me; but behold, Lemuel did think it would be better and more grammatical to call us the people of Laman or Lamanites; wherefore, I did agree, and we were thereafter called Lamanites.

19 Now, I did more than once hear some of the children of my brother refer to themselves as Lemuelites, and the children of the sons of Ishmael as Ishmaelites; but behold, I did remind them that the name,

Ishmaelites, was already spoken for by Abraham's posterity through his concubine, Hagar, and that they would know this if they had studied their genealogy; wherefore, they did remind me that we no longer had the brass plates and had become genealogically challenged.

20 But behold, the family of the exchange student did not complain, for their name was one of those funny ones with lots of consonants and no vowels and nobody could pronounce it anyway; wherefore, nothing was even named after them, so they were happy to be called Lamanites and did give me no grief.

CHAPTER 20

Laman becomes king—He gives a glimpse of his laws and government—Being a king is no piece of cake—The government grows like Topsy.

AND it came to pass that I, Laman, did set up shop as the king over the Lamanites, and my first order of business was to impose a few stiff taxes; but behold, Lemuel did think that I should devise some laws first and then lay a tax on the people, for if there is no law, there could be no transgression of the law, as our father had taught us.

2 Now behold, I do not give a full account of all of my trendy and up-to-date laws, for I did remodel most of the musty old codes that were about as ancient as Melthusedick, nor do I tell of our nifty form of government, neither do I explain the laws of political science that Lemuel did help me invent, for I have written about all those things in my secret diary.

3 But behold, I did think that Moses was on the right track in a few cases; wherefore, I did pinch some of his ideas; yea, I did like his number five about humoring thy father and thy mother, for I was now a father and did notice that my own children did sometimes stumble with this item, for they did often make fun of my clothes and laugh at my taste in music and complain that I had a bad sense of direction, so I did throw in number five along with all my dandy new laws.

4 Now behold, I did soon learn that it was not all purple and fine linen to be a king; for behold, I did find myself tossing and turning over direct and indirect taxes, over progressive and graduated taxes, surtaxes and subtaxes, and flat taxes and round taxes; wherefore, I did murmur unto Lemuel that this job was the pits and that it did give me insomnia and also kept me awake.

5 But Lemuel did try to cheer me up, saying that all kings had their bad days, and he did quote the ancient scripture wherein it says: Uneasy lies the head that wears the crown; but behold, I did remind Lemuel that I did not even own a crown yet, and even if I did, I certainly wouldn't be dumb enuf to sleep in it.

6 And it came to pass that Lemuel did help me by inventing several especially hefty assessments, including a three percent sales tax to raise money for the crown that I decided to

wear, thanks to the suggestion of my brother; yea, I did not wish to enter the first year of my administration shorthanded or bareheaded.

7 Now behold, some of my people did think that I should work like everybody else, but it did not seem right to me that the king should put in all of the late hours and lose all of the sleep that a king must lose, then fret and fume about his people and about all of the taxes he has to saddle them with, and to worry himself sick that the Lord might up and lead off some other poor, unsuspecting chosen people and plop them down right in our own backyard, yea, and do all of the other nail-biting and sleep-disturbing things that a king must do, and then go out and fetch himself a second job!

8 And it came to pass that I did not listen to the small-minded views of my people, and I did remind them that they were now living in a monarchy, and that we would not have a representative government for about twenty-five hundred years.

9 And behold, my duties as the king began to be exceedingly heavy; wherefore, I did hire Lemuel full time, that he might be the vice king; yea, and we did employ others to be our cabinet and our counselors and still others to be their assistants and then a bevy of secretaries to keep track of all the appointments and the paperwork created by the assistants and the counselors and the cabinet.

10 And it came to pass that we did need a whole department just to collect the taxes; yea and another to maintain the tax rolls and still another to help spend the taxes; and behold, Lemuel was happy that we had become a numerous people, for the government had become our number one growth industry.

CHAPTER 21

Moron is sent to spy upon the people of Nephi—The bad news is that they have become prosperous—The worse news is that they have armed themselves to the teeth—Lemuel sends out the first draft notice in the promised land, and the Lamanites raise their own army.

NOW behold, I, Laman, did begin to ponder somewhat upon the fate of Nephi and the others who had wandered off, for no matter how busy a king gets, he finds time to worry; yea, and I did begin to grow uneasy, for I did not have a very trusting nature; wherefore, I did wonder if these nomads might not come slinking back on some dark and stormy night to snitch some of the seeds they had left behind or help themselves to the gold and silver and precious things we had started to pile up.

2 And it came to pass that I did send a spy party into the wilderness, and Moron, my eldest son, did go at the head of this party; but behold, Lemuel did have a saying: Like father, like son; wherefore, he did take Moron aside to remind him that we did use the word "party" figuratively and that he was not to traipse off into the bush just to kick up his heels.

3 And it came to pass that after many days the scouting

party did return, and they were tired and dirty and hungry and out of sorts, and Moron did say that it was the furthest thing from a real party that he could remember, for they had been lost twice, and they had run out of food, and everywhere the water was bad; wherefore, most of them did come down with Montezuma's revenge; yea, and the wilderness was just swarming with insects, and Moron was stung right between the eyes by a thing called a deseret; and behold, his face did swell up so much that his eyes went shut; wherefore, he had to be led most of the way home.

4 And behold, this was just the good news, for the spies did tell us that they had found the people of Nephi, who had taken upon themselves the name of Nephites, which Lemuel thought was a possible copyright infringement; yea, and what's more, they had become very prosperous, for they had planted their seeds instead of keeping them in barrels as we had done, and they did reap abundant crops, and they did have many flocks and herds and animals of every kind; yea, they did even have a handy new animal like unto a camel, save it was smaller and friendlier and did not spit.

5 And behold, the people of Nephi did erect many buildings of wood and stone and iron and copper and other metals that Sam must have invented; yea, and this was not all, for they had built a beautiful temple, and it was ornamented with gold and silver and you guessed it; wherefore, it did make our little encampment look like a dump.

6 Now behold, there was still more bad news, for these same Nephites were armed; yea, they did all wear swords like unto the sword of that war-monger Laban, for Moron did borrow one that had been left under a tree by a careless Nephite; wherefore, he did bring it back for all to see.

7 Yea, I did now find another reason to dislike that expired tub-o'-lard Laban, and I did figure out why my brother, Nephi, did swipe that sword when he left; yea, he did wish to go into the sword-building business and needed a good prototype; wherefore, I did cuss Lemuel for not thinking of this idea first and letting Nephi get the drop on us.

8 Now behold, this was all grim news unto me, for a king does not like to hear that the kingdom next door is cavorting in the lap of luxury; yea, I had spread the rumor that Nephi and his gang were off wading somewhere knee-deep in misery, while we were camped on easy street; but behold, now they would learn that the Nephites had somehow struck oil, and I did worry that they might think we were living at low water and were nothing but poor, swarthy trash, and all because of their king who wouldn't take another job since he was too busy working full-time inventing taxes; yea, I did smell a mutiny.

9 Now, it was a funny thing, but one day we were all as happy as clams, as satisfied and content and comfortable as

a Bedouin in a bed, and the next day, just as soon as we did learn that somebody else was living flush, we did get grumpy and dissatisfied and just full of misery; yea, and what stuck in my craw was the news that the Nephites were armed to the teeth, for it did show a deep lack of trust in their neighbors and did reflect badly upon me and my people.

10 Wherefore, I did call together my vice king and my cabinet and my counselors and my administrators and especially my spin doctors, that we might figure out a way to take matters in hand and put our best foot forward.

11 And behold, Lemuel, bless his hardened heart, did truly understand the political process; wherefore, he did propose that we organize our own army, that we might defend ourselves and also keep the people occupied; yea, if we had an army we would need a whole mess of soldiers, with captains and lootenants and generals, and gobs of people helping the war effort behind the lines, which would stimulate the economy something fierce; yea, and we could even crank out some nice new war taxes and slap heavy duties on all of those war-time products that might be in short supply; wherefore, we would keep the home front humming along and let the army go off to do what an army does best, namely plundering.

12 And it came to pass that we did set about to build up our arsenal, for we did turn our plowshares into swords, which was one way to get out of farming; yea, we did fashion scimitars and bows and arrows and clubs and knives and forks, for we did seek to create a great army that was just bristling with weapons like unto the Nephites.

13 But behold, to my surprise, no one did wish to join our army; yea, we were up to our ears in firepower, but we did have only three applicants, and they were all for the job of general; wherefore, Lemuel did suggest that we compel the people to serve in the army, like unto the Babylonians and Philistines and all the best marauders.

14 And it came to pass that Lemuel did write a letter that we did mail out to all of those fit to be in our army, and Lemuel did say that its purpose was to impress people; and behold, I did think it was a beautiful letter, and I did know that everyone else would be exceedingly impressed, for it did begin warm and friendly like, saying: Behold, Uncle Laman Wants You!

15 But behold, to our great surprise, nobody rushed forward to join; yea, it was harder than we did imagine to force people to sign up; wherefore, I did cogitate for days trying to think of ways to make people catch the old *espree da coor*; and behold, I did hit upon the perfect scheme, for I did propose that anybody who did sign up would not have to milk cows or thin beets; yea, and I did offer to give them a bonus of twenty-five percent of the plunder; but behold, Lemuel said I was giving away the store; wherefore, he did reduce the

amount to a ten percent gratuity.

16 Now behold, it did work like a charm, and at last we did raise an army of thirty-seven soldiers, mostly young boys, and they did sign on the dotted line, and we did issue each of them a tin dog-tag, a sword, and a packet of MREs.

CHAPTER 22

The Lamanites become a pain in the neck unto the Nephites—Missionaries come among the Lamanites—Two of the sons of Laman convert—Laman laments the loss of his sons and recounts the sorrow of a wicked father whose sons turn against him in righteousness—The tin plates are full—Laman turns them over to Moron, who heads north to California.

AND it came to pass that we did send our army against the people of Nephi with Moron as our general, that we might carry off some of their excess flocks and herds and snake away some of the surplus of their crops, for their seeds must have been better than ours; yea, our seeds, when we got around to planting them, did produce crops that were just so-so; but behold, Lemuel did contend that we did not plant our seeds when the moon was right, but I think that our seeds got moldy on our long cruise, or maybe we just got gypped with an inferior brand.

2 Now behold, our army did enjoy looting and took delight in plundering; yea, it was much easier to rustle the flocks and herds of the Nephites than to raise our own; and behold, it was also more fun, especially after we learned to ride those wild horses without getting bucked off.

3 Now the Nephites did begin to speak of us as a loathsome, wicked, and stiff-necked people, and did call us bloodthirsty and idolatrous; wherefore, I did take great offense at such sloppy generalities, for I did not think that we were loathsome.

4 And it came to pass that more and more of the Lamanites did join the army and leave the farm, for we were doing a brisk business; yea, we did become a great pain in the neck unto the Nephites, which did warm my heart, for there is no greater satisfaction than to be an instrument in the re-distribution of the wealth of somebody else.

5 Now behold, some of our women did wish to go out and join in the looting, for the army did seem to be having a grand old time of it while the women stayed home and did the chores; but behold, I did steadfastly refuse to allow women in the military; yea, Lemuel did counsel that women would soon lose their soft and cuddly natures and would become fierce and bloodthirsty; wherefore, I did calm the waters by telling the women that we could not afford to build separate barracks; yea, and Lemuel did promise to drag Nephi's boat out of mothballs and to take them all on a little vacation to the Caribbean once we finished with the marauding and the war slacked off.

6 And it came to pass that from time to time we did have

"And our subjects did honor us with large statues of their king and vice king, but they were not a good likeness, for my lips were too big and Lemuel's head was too pointy."

missionaries from the Nephites, and they did come among us and did preach unto us and did pray for us and did hold cottage meetings; yea, they did try to turn the Lamanites from the wicked traditions of their fathers, which I did think was a slap in the face unto Lemuel and me, neither could I think of one single tradition that I, or Lemuel either, had invented; wherefore, I did clap them into one of my spare prisons.

7 But behold, they were such nice boys, clean-cut and polite, that I did let them off with just a few months in the slammer after I did admonish them to go easy on the wicked traditions bit; yea, for they began to sound too much like unto my father, Lehi, when he bit off more than he could chew back in Jerusalem; and I did warn them that if they were not careful, the Lord might decide to adopt them as his chosen people; and behold, it was a sure bet that if he glommed onto them, in no time flat they would be hitting the road to some gold-forsaken wilderness for a couple of decades and then end up in a promised land that didn't even have bicycles.

8 And it came to pass that there was great sadness in our family, for two of my own sons, Modicum and Gazebo, did convert and follow after the teachings of the missionaries; wherefore, I did grieve much for the apostasy of my sons, for there is no pain like unto that of a wicked father whose sons turn against him in righteousness; yea, I did know how old Faro felt when Moses, who was like a son unto him and had been spoiled by him, did up and leave home, taking all of his union bricklayers with him, which set the pyramids back considerable.

9 And behold, I did warn my other children against the dangers of cults, and I did plead with them to be wary of the teachings of the elders; for behold, they could surely end up spending their entire days in doing good and being kind; wherefore, they would soon degenerate into a white and delightsome people and forget their rich idolatrous heritage and be no more a stiff-necked and bloodthirsty people; yea, they would probably even take up genealogy maybe, and start reading the brass plates and ramble on about Isaiah.

10 Now behold, my other children did remain true and faithful unto the principles we had taught them; wherefore, they did stay strong and proud, relying upon the arm of flesh; yea, they were not weak like unto those wimpy Nephites, who did depend upon the Lord for help; for the Lamanites did not ask the Lord for one plug nickel, neither of anyone else, for no sooner does the Lord or anybody else do you a favor than they want to be paid back, with interest.

11 And Lemuel did support me in this, for he did tell our people that they should not go looking around for a free lunch or for handouts from the government, either; yea, they should not ask what their country could do for them, but what they could do for their country, which sounded real good and kept the

LAMAN 22:12-18

enlistments up and the taxes flowing.

12 Now behold, I did have many other wise teachings, for I had become a popular king among my people, although Lemuel did remind me that there were no other kings for comparison, since Zedekiah was about a million miles away and most of the children had never heard of him anyway, but then Lemuel was always a little ticked that he was only the vice king.

13 But behold, my favorite teachings and wise sayings and ruminations upon life I have recorded in my secret diary; and behold, I did enlighten my people, with Lemuel chipping in now and then with some of his kooky ideas; wherefore, my subjects did honor me with a large statue to their king, but it did seem to me that the head was exceedingly large and the face was not a good likeness, for the lips were too big and the eyes squinty.

14 Now behold, Morona did tell me to record upon these plates all of our children, for they are nearly full (the plates, not my children); and behold, the names of my seed are these, beginning with my sons: Moron, Egad, Modicum, Scrimshaw, Gazebo, Kokapelli, little Sharem, and the baby Juan Valdez; and my daughters are Babylonia, Gonorrah, Reebok, Santuccia, and Agonia, plus, of course, the twins, Dan and Beersheba.

15 And it came to pass that I began to be old, and it did seem to happen overnight; yea, I did wake up one morning feeling tired and achy, and when I did glance into the mirror, behold, there was an old man looking back at me; wherefore, I did immediately call my son, Moron, unto me, that I might give him charge concerning the plates of tin whereupon I have inscribed my account.

16 And behold, I did confer upon him the record of our people, and I did command him that he should keep the record, that it might someday come forth unto our seed, and I did remind him again that this was merely a figurative way of speaking about children that I had learned from my father, that our posterior may some day know my side of the story; yea, and that they may know of my trials and afflictions and tribulations and adversities and in general the lousy time I had during our wanderings in the wilderness, led by a visionary father and a nearly perfect brother, and I do not mean Lemuel!

17 And it came to pass that Moron did give me the shock of my life; yea, he did inform me that he had decided to take an early retirement from the army, with full pension, of course, before he ended up on the wrong end of a sword held by some distraught Nephite who had lost his cows; wherefore, he had decided to visit the land northward beyond the narrow neck of land; and behold, he planned to take his family and a few friends with him; yea, they might even settle in California or Oregon if it wasn't too crowded.

18 But behold, he did consent to take my roof, that is the tin

plates, with him, and did agree to guard the record with his life, tho he hoped it would not come to that.

19 Now I, Laman, did worry about this trip, for Moron was lousy with directions, having inherited a healthy dose of those wandering chromosomes that afflicted his uncle Nephi and his grandfather Lehi; wherefore, I did fear that he might miss the beautiful beaches and fertile valleys along the coast, and that he would meander off and end up in some place with gobs of desert and endless sagebrush and salty water, like Utah.

20 But behold, I, Laman, am growing old and tired, and I do not wish to worry about these infernal plates any more, and if I had known how much trouble it would be to inscribe our story upon them, I would have let Nephi have the field to himself.

21 And behold, the plates are full, and I do write on the last few inches of tin before turning them over to Moron, and whether they will ever survive the trip north, I know not; yea, I do know that once we remove the tin plates from our roof that Morona will be yelling at me to put up another one before the rainy season.

22 Now behold, if you wish to learn more about our wanderings and about our life in the promised land, you may look for my secret diary, which I did give unto my musical son, Kokapelli, or you might consult *The Little Book of Lemuel*, but his account should be taken with a grain of salt, for he did have some of the nuttiest ideas, being a middle child; and behold, he was always way too metaphorical for my taste; yea, I did quite often suspect that with Lemuel, too much sand had blown over the dune.

23 And behold, one last word of advice: Do not pay any attention to dreams that start out with marching orders like Hit the Road, Jack, or Get Out of Town; for behold, you could just wind up a long way from nowhere in a whole heap of trouble.

THEE END